Trumped

Trumped

Poets Speak (while we still can), vol. 1

Edited by John Roche

Beatlick Press
&
Jules' Poetry Playhouse Publications
Albuquerque, NM

Poets Speak (while we still can) is a series of mini-anthologies addressing the current national and planetary crisis.

Series Editor: John Roche
Associate Editor: Jules Nyquist
Art Editor: Denise Weaver Ross

Cover Design: Denise Weaver Ross
Interior Illustration: Michael Young, "Trumped"
(Grayscale version of the color original)
Interior Illustration: Larry Goodell, "Speech Control Incorporated"
(Grayscale)

Special thanks to Beatlick Press publisher Pamela Adams Hirst and Beatlick Press editor Deborah Woodside Coy.

ISBN-13: 978-1544737508
ISBN-10: 1544737505
Printed in the United States of America

All copyrights remain with the authors, artists and photographers

Copyright ©2017 Beatlick Press and Jules' Poetry Playhouse Publications, all rights reserved.

Acknowledgments

The following poems have appeared elsewhere:

Mikki Aronoff's "Q Does as Q Likes at the Sugar Bun & Elsewhere" appeared in *Rise Up Review*, Jan. 2017.

G.L. Brower's "Autumn in the Bosque, Winter in America (2016)" appeared in the chapbook *Autumn Gifts/Winter Treasures*, Las Placitas Presbyterian Church, Placitas, NM, 2016.

Tony Brown's "Our Dragon," appeared on his poetry blog, "Dark Matter," found at radioactiveart.wordpress.com

Dee Cohen's "Wolves" appeared in *Adobe Walls* Dec. 2010.

Alan Kaufman's "Let Us" appeared in *The Villager*, Dec. 2016.

Ezra E. Lipschitz's "Eulogy" appeared in his book, *I Shouldn't Say: The Mostly Unedited Poems of Ezra E. Lipschitz*, Mezcalita Press, 2017.

Colleen Powderly's poem "Grief" appeared in *California Quarterly 31:2 2005*, and in *Studio One 2005*.

John Roche's "Trumped" appeared in *Talkers of the Town* blogspot talkersofthetown.com, Oct. 2016, and also in *Duke City Fix*, dukecityfix.com

Scott Wiggerman's "Aftershocks" appeared in *Transition: Poems in the Aftermath*, Indolent Books blogsite, 28 Nov. 2016. www.indolentbooks.com

Michael Young, *Trump*

Preface

Trumped is volume one of *Poets Speak (while we still can)*, a series of anthologies in response to the national and planetary crisis provoked by the election of 11/8/16. Forthcoming 2017 volumes are to be titled *Hers, Water, Survival,* and *Walls*.

The editors envision these mini-anthologies as rapid responses in the tradition of Medieval and Renaissance broadsides, Tom Paine's pamphlets, Walt Whitman's *The 18th President* and *Democratic Vistas*, Emanuel Haldeman-Julius's Blue Books, the IWW Songbook, the A.J. Muste Memorial pamphlet series, and Samizdat dissident publications from behind the Iron Curtain.

Any profits arising from this series will be donated to the following organizations:
The Southwest Women's Law Center, the American Civil Liberties Union, the Southern Poverty Law Center, the National Immigration Law Center, and the Indigenous Environmental Network.

We wish to thank all the poets and artists who are contributing to this project! And to the series subscribers!

Submission and subscription information can be found here:
http://www.julesnyquist.com/submissions-poets-speak-.html

Another World Is Possible!

¡Sí, Se Puede!

Contents

I.
1. John Roche, *Trumped*
3. Teresa Mei Chuc, *After Trump*
4. Mary Strong Jackson, *His Orangeness*
5. George Wallace, *From the Back of Your Throat Come Devils and Landlords*
6. George Wallace, *It's Springtime in America, Fuck You Is in the Air*
7. Djelloul Marbrook, *Trump Goes with Tricks*
8. Bobbie Lee Lovell, *The Candidate*
9. Maril Nowak, *Bloviation*
10. Mikki Aronoff, *Q Does as Q Likes at the Sugar Bun & Elsewhere*
12. Susy Crandall, *Trump Blows*
13. Deborah Coy, *Infinite Trumps*
15. Larry Belle, *President @realDonaldTrump*
18. Megan Baldrige, *Preschool Progress Report*
20. Catherine Iselin, *Primaries Pantoum*
21. Vincent F. A. Golphin, *Love Trumped*
22. Michael Ketchek, *Trump's America Song*
23. Mary Ellen Kelly, *Who Country*
24. Eleanor Grogg Stewart, *A Golf Course in Scotland*
25. Douglas Lipton, *Donald, Where's Your Visa, or Hope Against Hope*
26. Stuart A. Paterson, *Immigration Visa No. 26698, New York, May 11th 1930*
27. Stephen Lackow, *Under Development*

II.
32. Michael Rothenberg, *We Turned the Universe*
34. Eugene Stelzig, *Things Unthinkable*
35. Dee Cohen, *Wolves*
36. Scott Wiggerman, *Aftershocks*
37. Gretchen Schulz, *deluge*
38. Patrick Colm Hogan, from *Travels in the Land of Pious Men*
39. Jared Smith, *Something Dark Beyond Words*
40. John Berry, *The Day Before It's Official*
41. G.L. Brower, *Autumn in the Bosque, Winter in America (2016)*
43. Randy Prus, *The Potomac by Moonlight*
44. Jim Cohn, *Cold Moon*

45.	Colleen Powderly, *Grief: November 9, 2016*	
46.	Fred Whitehead, *Remorse*	
47.	Jim Cohn, *This Week*	
48	Terez Peipins, *As a Trumpet Warns*	
49.	John Roche, *A Funeral Procession on Pennsylvania Avenue (January 20, 2017)*	
50.	Ezra E. Lipschitz, *Eulogy*	

III.

52.	Mary Dudley, *How We Got Here*
53.	Jack Bradigan Spula, *Ballad of the Ballots*
55.	Steve Coffman, *Making Our Move*
56.	Steve Ausherman, *We Bind Our Own Feet*
57.	Patricia Roth Schwartz, *Know Better*
58.	Lalita Pandit Hogan, *Of Blue*
59.	David Morse, *Splitting a Crow's Tongue*
60.	Larry Goodell, *Us is U.S.*
62.	Holly Wilson, *All Umped Up and Nowhere to Go*
63.	Gayle Lauradunn, *Tribal Shorts*
64.	Kathamann, *Maybe This Is Why*
65.	Joe Weil, *Red State Polka*
66.	Randy Prus, *Red State Blues*
67.	Sylvia Ramos Cruz, *Post-outrage*
69.	Ceinwen E. C. Haydon, *And*
70.	Dennis Maloney, **from** *The Faces of Guan Yin*

IV.

72.	Jules Nyquist, *Zozobra and the Hallelujah Chorus*
73.	Jack Hirschman, *The Ashes of Nada Arcane*
77.	Michael Peters, *Excerpts from "O Beautiful Death™: A Rage Device Index"*
80.	Rudy Rucker, *The Third Bomb*
85.	Tony Brown, *Our Dragon*
87.	Kitty Jospé, *No Trump*
88.	Bruce Bennett, *Our Rough Beast*
89.	Pris Campbell, *Heading South*
90.	Gregory L. Candela, *Trumpet of God*

V.

92.	Caitlin Gildrien, *Transition*
94.	Alan Kaufman, *Let Us (For the Poets of January 15 and the Women of January 21st)*
95.	Gino Sky, *Ommmmmm Mani Safety Pin Hummmmm*
96.	A. D. Winans, *Trump Land*
97.	Margaret Randall, *Nothing at All to Learn*
98.	Michael C. Ford, *Martyred Saints*
99.	Kenneth Gurney, *Blowing Steam 18 Dec 2016*
101.	Larry Goodell, *Buy Free Speech*
102.	Jim Fish, *Election 2016*
103.	Dick Bakken, *Star Spangle Banter*
104.	Steven Deridder, *Supercharge*
107.	Bill Nevins, *Fascist Religions Make You Feel So GOOD*
108.	Neil Young, *In Praise of Hecklers*
109.	Fred Whitehead, *The Eighth of November*
110.	Don Paul, *We Hold the Cards for an Old and New Way*
112.	Joe Weil, *Poem at Thanksgiving, 2016*
113.	Ed Sanders, *Broom Poem*
114.	Ed Sanders, *What to Do?*

Addenda.

116.	*An Anti-Inaugural Masque*
120.	Bios
131.	Publishers' Page

I.

John Roche

Trumped

Trump looms
Trump lurks
Trump snorts

Trump humps the chair
Trump grasps the electric sceptre
Trump pants and groans
Trump sweats orange bleeds orange melts orange

No mad Sweeney
No mad Lear
No mad Queeg
How can a brand be mad?
How can a brand be tragic?
How can a brand be a man?

Trump Steaks
Trump hotels
Trump casinos
"Success by Trump" cologne
The Trump Shuttle
Trump neckwear
Trump cufflinks
Trump chandeliers
Trump cocktail tables
Trump barstools
Trump Vodka
Trump Natural Spring Water
Trump Ice-- yes, he really tried to market ice!
Trump the Game
Trump University
Tour de Trump

A nation of salesmen meets the age of simulacra
The ultimate Babbitt
The true fruition of everything Melville, Twain,
Whitman, Veblen, Lewis, Vidal warned us against

The Donald 'R' US
In Hype We Trust

All of us coated with a great orange oil slick
All of us covered in the gurry of it, as Olson would say
All of us covered in great orange whale shit

Is it possible to write poetry after Trump?

Teresa Mei Chuc

After Trump

we are learning to walk again
as if for the first time
and to talk with each other

take an unsteady step towards
the open arms of our humanity

Mary Strong Jackson

His Orangeness

if sin has a smell   the air stinks of it
try and push it from your nostrils
snort like a bull   still it stays
like cattle stink from feedlots
it's called the "smell of money"

his Orangeness drops stink
as he sings one line by a songwriter
he can't name, "This Land is MY Land"
his tours emit nastinesses that drug his followers
they drop to their knees when they read
5 giant letters on an airplane or a building

he passes oranges to the working class
the fruit rots at his touch
he says it doesn't and hands spoiled fruit
like gifts to open hands

George Wallace

From the Back of Your Throat Come Devils and Landlords

& what is this strange ointment, this dubious trill of a Queens canary, this handwrit promissory note, uncollectible, bust up the string quartet why don't you,

Make a fool of old shovelfoot, kneel down on the throat of the slide trombone, climb on top you twitterheaded tanktop eraser, you piping hot lie machine -- melt down microphone

Yes yes I have heard the deep bop of your new flambeau, it fools everyone, must've learned that in a tv script or straight from Putin –

And yes, you strapped-on uptown tight-lipped motherfucker, tossing matches into the gas tank of America to see what's what

Inflammatory racketeer dressed in scorchers, nomad seductor

From the back of your throat come devils and landlords, dressed in the latest demon demoiselles, this sinuous accountancy, a factorial zero in the mink,

Nubile, erect, cantering puttyfinger, pussy grabbing nobody jacked up like a star

O eminent domain discount narcissus

O heavenly trinket, self-declared, the root of my pain, I feel you in my spine

O let down your hair, unglamorous warrior

George Wallace

It's Springtime in America, Fuck You Is in the Air

Trump Tower New York City the pleasant little solitaire the bold lonely penthouse gestures all the sexy stock options and stupid surprises on every platform and corner a proposition for you dear everywhere you look like a turnstile of love you look like the crosshairs of money

A revolving door of indices and economic indicators what ails you, my girl my girl

You are one lucky sonofabitch living on the top floor in the meatwheel of America New York New York uneasy oasis of jerkweed Coca Cola and look at your name in every windowpane a newminted coin in your mouth a sensational woman to prod

You got the big chromium smile you! You got the smart ridiculous rollsuit you! Idiot, not to mention in a big damn hurry

O mister pocketpants with your poppa's money to throw around, your hookers and slaves your stink of knock-off French perfume, your snap on cheap ass pay your bill pussy tree -- rev it up screw it down piss it out on cobblestones

The rainbow shines for you o shaky breaky nastyman. Meet me by the unlisted telephone number. With rage all right. With deals all right.

Huge deals.
Bum deals.

Choke it back thrust it out let's get it done.

Djelloul Marbrook

Trump Goes with Tricks

When did we ever have a more aptly named president? The verb trump means to beat, and beating and getting over on someone is the new president's biography in a nutshell. But as a policy the verb is fraught with danger, because the beaten learn and the gotten over on get up and fight back. We were trumped at Pearl Harbor... you know the end of that story. And in playing cards and Tarot trump goes with tricks.

Bobbie Lee Lovell

The Candidate

His name is the sound
of an angry fist slammed hard
on a lectern. What

does this billionaire
know of your life, your struggle?
Don't let him buy you.

Don't let him buy back
his own hostile words. What else
would this man erase?

Your reality
is not his reality
show. So stop watching.

Tune in to your own
heart, the inner voice he lacks
that says: Not like this.

Hate will never be
the lesser of two evils.
Masked as ignorance,

patriotism
or generalization,
it all stinks the same.

Maril Nowak

Bloviation

H.L. Mencken once said, "[President Harding] writes the worst English
I have ever encountered:
…a string of wet noodles
…tattered washing on the line
…stale bean soup
…college yells
…dogs barking idiotically through endless nights.
It is so bad that a sort of grandeur creeps into it. It drags itself out of
the dark abysm of pish, and crawls insanely up the topmost pinnacle of
posh. It is rumble and bumble. It is flap and doodle. It is balder and
dash."

Not since Warren Harding (was he also an insomniac?),
who never had the luxury of midnight Twitter,
have we had such a Bloviator-in-Chief.
Our 2017 president-elect is a screeching bird of prey
in a frenetic search for its own brain.

While democracy survived Harding,
the Donald's "huge" legacy is still being written
in third-grade-level vocabulary and
abbreviated quacks that already make nations,
industries, families, teachers and poets tremble.

Mikki Aronoff

Q Does as Q Likes at the Sugar Bun & Elsewhere

I'm an ass with a tail,
a t/rump, an unrelenting
Ouroborus gone south,
strut-waddling like
Scrooge McDuck.
I'm greased like Porky,
get what I grunt
and hunt for, learned
squeak 'n' sneak
early in the game,
my place in the litter
sandwiched
between P and R,
buxom runts. I said
runts. I favored R's
restless, skinny legs.
That pig squiggled
and squealed
for my divided attention,
my orange assets taunting.
Tabu dreams in a silk purse.
P was P, a bust on a stick,
my ultimate undoing,
my tight pants doomed
forever to follow my lust,
propel me out of bed every
morning at 3, the tweeting hour.
I snuffle to the elevator, ride
down the tower to the Sugar Bun,
my main vein, my very famous
yeasty mother lode. I light ovens
for the buns - like mine, always
on the rise, and ice
the Scrabble tile cookies,
all Q's, backsides labeled
100% Made in the USA.... Wrong!
The sweetness you smell?
Released by the shop door
closing down on a piece
of scratch 'n' sniff. I am

very smart and I've got every
thing you desperately want.
So get in line.
Fork over.

Susy Crandall

Trump Blows

The deepest darkness
inside contains galaxies
The world
that contains me
I contain
even as it
races out of
control committing
all the old atrocities
all over again.
The last Trump
blows
his horn
and promises us victory
in the old Teutonic
style,
and the
frightened
hordes are
only too eager
to jump on
his crazy
train.
"Make America great again!" they whine,
"Save us from the promises of the best of us,"
they cry, "the promises that make
less of us and more of them."
I have lived through this
before, I wonder how
I'll do it again.
I go inside the darkness
that contains galaxies
and see it all within me.

Deborah Coy

Infinite Trumps

I plucked a new timeline
every time I made a decision.
A resonance that got me here
to this particular parallel universe.

All that was fixed,
was before my birth.
I join the program in progress
as I swing on a new string
like Tarzan
collecting timelines as frequently
as I choose produce.

Somewhere, back then,
I chose a series of wrongs
that got me here
to this bizarro universe.
A place where Rupert Murdoch
marries Mick Jagger's ex,
a place where you can buy cheesy fries
for your dog for $14.99.
A place where we spend
more to kill people than to save them.

Should I have picked
the riper cantaloupe?
Would it have made a difference
if I chose paper instead of plastic?

Is there a universe
where Donald Trump's fame
was only worth fifteen minutes,
where George W. lost the election,
where 911 didn't happen
and we the people
still believed in civility?
I wonder what string
I could have pulled to get me there.

But now I live
in a universe of infinite Trumps.
Trumps on Facebook,
Trumps on the news,
small hand Trumps,
Trump's Cheeto penis.

I believe there is a universe
where Trump is just a dock worker
or died at birth,
or is just a small handed T Rex.

If I knew what vines
to swing from
I would high tail it
to another universe
where Trump
farts mightily
and destroys
the Republican party.

Larry Belle

President @realDonaldTrump

*It is by a thorough knowledge of the whole subject
that you are enabled to judge correctly of the past
and to give a proper direction to the future.*
James Monroe

You know, I'm, like, a smart person.
I don't have to be told the same thing
in the same words every single day
for the next eight years
If something should change, let me know.

*All the lessons of history and experience must
be lost upon us if we are content to trust alone
to the peculiar advantages we happen to possess.*
Martin VanBuren

I alone can fix it

*The storm of frenzy and faction must
inevitably dash itself in vain against
the unshaken rock of the Constitution.*
Franklin Pierce

I'm going to open up our libel laws
so when dishonest, scum, crooked journalists
write negative and horrible and false articles,
we can sue them and win lots of money.

*Better to remain silent and be thought a fool
than to speak out and remove all doubt.*
Abraham Lincoln

It's like in golf.
A lot of people—I don't want this to sound trivial—
but a lot of people are switching to these really long putters,
very unattractive. It's weird.
You see these great players with these really long putters, because
they can't sink three-footers anymore.
And I hate it. I am a traditionalist.

I have so many fabulous friends who happen to be
gay, but I am a traditionalist.

Older men declare war.
But it is youth that must fight and die.
And it is youth who must inherit
the tribulation, the sorrow and the triumphs
that are the aftermath of war.
Herbert Hoover

I would just bomb those suckers,
and that's right, I'd blow up the pipes,
I'd blow up the refineries,
I'd blow up every single inch,
there would be nothing left.
And you know what,
you'll get Exxon to come in there, and
in two months, you ever see these guys?
How good they are, the great oil companies,
they'll rebuild it brand new...
And I'll take the oil.

Piling up material goods cannot
fill the emptiness of lives which
have no confidence or purpose.
Jimmy Carter

I'm really rich.
That's the kind of mindset,
 that's the kind of thinking
you need for this country.

The future doesn't belong to the fainthearted;
it belongs to the brave.
Ronald Reagan

I had a doctor that gave me a letter —
a very strong letter on the heels,

If you live long enough,
you'll make mistakes.
But if you learn from them,
you'll be a better person.
William Clinton

Stay clear of women who "gripe" and "bitch."

*Other disputes have dragged on for weeks before
reaching resolution, and each time,
both the victor and the vanquished have accepted
the result peacefully and in a spirit of reconciliation.
So let it be with us.*
Albert Gore, Concession Speech

This whole election is being rigged.
The whole thing is one big fix.
One big ugly lie.
It's one big fix.

And the final word:
*No man will ever carry out of the Presidency
the reputation which carried him into it.*
Thomas Jefferson

And when you're a star they let you do it.
You can do anything ...
Grab them by the pussy.
You can do anything.

Megan Baldrige
       (with thanks to my sister Molly)

Preschool Progress Report
    To Mr. and Mrs. Trump:
    From his Preschool Teacher, Mrs. Brown
    Donald J. Trump's Preschool Progress Report, October 1950

Donald threatens to build a wall
to "keep Staten Island crybabies"
out of our preschool:
Claims he, alone,
can make his classroom great!

Donald refuses to share a cubby
with his cubby buddy, Juanito;
says he owns the boys' cubby area,
is willing to *rent* Juanito
that cubby,
then charges him double.

Donald doesn't try to color
inside the lines:
tries to pay Juanito
to do his coloring,
then does not pay him.

Donald refuses
to clean up after himself:
threatens Juanito
with deportation
unless Juanito cleans up for him.

Donald will not lie down
during naptime;
or, if pretending to sleep,
writes little notes insulting
"the fat girls."

Donald doesn't share blocks;
cannibalizes
Juanito's buildings,
adds a block,
calls them Trump towers.

Donald calls girls he doesn't like, "fat";
calls others, foxy."
The girls try to please him,
really mistrust him.

Donald explains
his hurtful comments to the girls
were taken out of context
by other kids,
especially by Juanita,
and by liberal girls.

Donald will not raise his hand
at circle time;
brings his own mic
uses it to talk OVER
other students, especially girls.

Donald refuses to practice the chorus for *Kumbaya*
with his classmates;
badgers me to turn the song
into a solo…for him.

Donald won't eat celery at snacktime;
has learned how to get
a cheeseburger delivered,
at recess.

Donald talks about
moving to the White House
sometime soon;
encourages Juanito to vote
for DONALD for President.

Donald tells Juanito
and the girls
he will never
vote for them, for President.

Donald tells me,
frequently,
"Teach,
You're fired!"

Catherine Iselin

Primaries Pantoum

The school-yard bullies are standing on stage
they look proper but are out of control
they exchange verbal punches
raise their fists and make faces.

They look proper but are out of control
the public is loud more like a mob
raise their fists and make faces
you hear a roar when insults fly by.

The public is loud more like a mob
roman times are back
you hear a roar when insults fly by
they all want blood.

Roman times are back
gladiators and lions have assembled
they all want blood
the coliseum is packed.

Gladiators and lions have assembled
they exchange verbal punches
the coliseum is packed
the school-yard bullies are standing on stage.

Vincent F. A. Golphin

Love Trumped

Fear is love trumped
a challenge to believe
that what the eyes tell us
is simply suspicion

Nov. 8 night lots of people watched
Blue States turn red, and electors' choices
trump their faith in a path toward a brighter day.
Like a child told that monsters do not exist,
the disaffected clung to billowy dreams, yet wondered
if insidious sights and sounds that loom over the dark road
ahead are true threats, or myths that slice at dreams
from which the fearful will awaken in the light

Fear is love trumped
a challenge to believe
that what the eyes tell us
is simply suspicion

That a president who is no politician can dish out
the bounteous fruits described in his populist predictions
that a cabinet of bosses will open doors for desperate, angry workers,
who trust in Trump's bold campaign proclamations
like kids on Christmas wait for Santa to fulfill their deepest desires.
Yet fear oozes into the cracks in their convictions.

Fear is love trumped
a challenge to believe
that what the eyes tell us
is simply suspicion

They see a Secretary of Education who does not favor public schools,
a Secretary for Housing that sees subsidized homes as handouts,
a Secretary of Energy who cannot recall the name of his department,
and a man in charge of labor who thinks the poor are paid too much.
Like children in night's blackness, the disappointed jump at shadows,
imagine that what appears in the darkness around them is fake,
imagine that goodness won't go on vacation, and face the untenable leap
to join those who blithely say, "Give him a chance,"
and disregard wisdom.

Michael Ketchek

Trump's America Song

Oh beautiful for smog-filled skies
And amber fields now fracked
Those purple mountains all chopped down
As much more coal is hacked

America, America
Give your money to me
And let rich white men prevail
From sea to shining sea

Mary Ellen Kelly

Who Country

Who is this country that voted for this man
Again and Again
even when this man turned his face into the camera
like a hungry animal of no specific breed
whose belly is full
but that doesn't matter
because he never has enough

Who is this man with a hunger to hurt
anyone in his way to the gold mountain

Where will this man go tomorrow
with his trophy of a whirling world turned upside down

Pick up the phone he repeats over and over again
Ring ring ring

Calls from leaders swallowing their own bile to say
Welcome to the club. Your room key is in the mail.
Meet you in the locker room.
See you at the first toast.
The first roast.
The unending boast.

Who takes this man for your lawful wedded leader
Who will follow him to the end of the earth
Who will watch him point his gun and pull the trigger for fun
Who will hand out the vests and helmets and dig the trenches
Who will take the children underground when he comes near
Who will cry for our country
Who knows how to stop the flood

When will you get on bended knee and beg forgiveness
from the woman who gave this country everything she had
When will you offer your hand
to help any other woman
any person who has never been white
rise up from those wet cold trenches
to face a man like this man ever again

Eleanor Grogg Stewart

A Golf Course in Scotland
>*(Based on the film "You've Been Trumped" by Anthony Baxter)*

Of course, he didn't care about the unique dunes
Much less an endangered snail
Has he ever even walked outside except on a golf course?

But the people--the Scottish people who lived there
Didn't they have rights?
Didn't they matter?
He saw them as an eyesore ruining the high-rise view
From his hotel-to-be
He called the farm a junkyard—an old working farm
And he tried to force them off their ancestral land

One day no electricity—next would be their water
When asked on camera, he said, "Who cares? Nobody cares"
But their neighbors did and city people marched to help them
It looked bad on the news so he turned it all back on again
And built a wall instead
A wall of berm so high--"a beautiful wall"

The old woman said, "He doesn't want us to see the golf course"
She didn't understand he didn't want the golf course to see her
It opened and he slouched behind the bagpipers like a monarch
And didn't notice that the golf balls thrown from the sidelines
Had swastikas on them

Douglas Lipton

Donald, Where's Your Visa, or Hope Against Hope
> *(regarding the controversial 2016 US Presidential election campaign and the proposal that its victor make an early visit to the U.K.)*

Let the wind blow high, let the wind blow low,
Through the streets with my quiff I go.
All the lassies say, "Hello,
Donald, where's your visa?"

Let the wind blow high, let the wind blow low,
Up to the head of the queue I go,
But the man at the desk says; "Oh, no, no,
Donald, where's your visa?"

"Inciting hatred; spreading fear —
Oh, Donald, you're not welcome here.
This country still holds some things dear.
Donald, where's your visa?"

I'm going to be the President.
A man like me is heaven-sent.
Just said some things I never meant.
"Donald, where's your visa?"

"We don't allow fomenters in,
Or bigots spouting words of sin,
So we're not going to let you in.
Donald, you've no visa."

They won't let me in to the old U.K.
Just because of the things I say.
I never meant to cause dismay.
"Donald, you've no visa."

Let the wind blow high, let the wind blow low,
Through the streets with my quiff I go.
All the lassies say, "Hello,
Donald, where's your visa?"

(apologies to Andy Stewart & Neil Grant)

Stuart A. Paterson

Immigration Visa No. 26698, New York, May 11th 1930

Mary Anne MacLeod, low-earning migrant
fleeing poverty to live with your sister
who'd been banished from a strict religious
land in an unwed childbirth scandal
just a few years previously, welcome to
America where thirteen years from now
you will yourself be wed, to Fred,
give birth to irony, or as he'll come
to soon be known, The Dómhnall.
Good job that Hoover isn't into building
walls, Mary Anne MacLeod from Croft 5
in Tong on Lewis, away in you come,
put your feet up, we'll make you a cup of tea
& have a chat about acceptance,
tolerance & the land of the fucking free.

Stephen Lackow

Under Development

Jamaica Estates was behind the gates
in Queens,
there was nothing there
but houses, mansions really
different than Belmont Avenue in East New York
where I was born, and lived,
even different than Pitkin Avenue
where the Trumps shopped for what they needed.

Pitkin Avenue was across the border
in Brooklyn,
but it might as well have been Another Country,
maybe another planet from Jamaica Estates –
only five miles away.
The Trumps loved meat, and they bought their meat
from a kosher butcher on Pitkin Avenue,
my Grandpa Benny.
You could build a whole week
around the Trump's meat order,
they had a lot of kids.
We thought Fred was a helluva guy.
Donald? Little Lord Fauntleroy,
Just another spoiled rich kid.

Years later, the Trumps finally moved to Brooklyn.
It was called "The Trump Organization."
It was down on Avenue Z
where, we heard, Fred was building swell new apartments
for working people like us.
Imagine that, it was too good to be true...

And it was.
Fred Trump forced some friends of our family
from their home,
into some crummy summer bungalow
all the way out on the tip of Coney Island
so he could build the Trump Village.
It was freezing there in the winter,
you could see breath before faces,
you were out in the cold.

Electric space heaters didn't do much.
One very cold night a heater caught fire
as they slept and burned their bungalow down –
almost all the bungalows burned down –
and they died.
Then, in some ramshackle apartment house down there,
my friend Bobby was sliding down the bannister
when the whole stairway collapsed.
From that day, we were reminded
what happened to Bobby.
What happens when you slide down the bannister, boys?
You end up in the hospital, like Bobby.
Oh, no, Bobby died.

Then, the City of New York would not let Fred Trump
turn our beloved Steeplechase Park –
to be a National Historic Place –
into Miami Beach high rises.
It is zoned for amusement, please develop amusement.
Fred Trump gave us amusement.
He invited everybody down to the Steeplechase
to knock the teeth out of the smiling clown
that had welcomed children of all ages, for generations,
with bricks and rocks and whatever they could find.
People emptied from the subway at Stillwell Avenue
and destroyed our past for one man's spite.

Then we found Fred Trump had polluted the Coney Island Creek
to build his Trump Village.
Coney Island Creek!
That Fred Trump nearly killed as dead as the Yellow Submarine there, sinking.
Coney Island Creek, that emptied onto Shell Road
beneath the creaking Culver line
where The Trake parked his hot dog truck
down by our little league.

II

Everybody called him The Trake
but not us,
my mother would never allow it.
The League made him park his rusty old truck
under the El all the way out on Shell Road, almost to the Aquarium,

so he wouldn't scare all the little kids
with the big hole in his throat.
But I know how I felt, I felt bad, very bad.
It was all mom could afford
to take my brother and me to The Trake for a hot dog.
Once in a while,
we kept right on going
all the way to Coney Island, 'til That
became sad, very sad,
too sad to be true, and too true not to be sad.
Closed the 'Chase,
the Cyclone stopped,
no Wonder
Wheel, the Coney Island of the Heart departed
for Jersey, for "The Island" – Long, not Coney, long
as our faces,
and in every window there was a switchblade knife.

Then, one day, Gil Hodges came.
He
walked all the way down Shell Road from his namesake field
to the rusty old truck, to The Trake -
with me trailing like a Lilliputian
but I didn't think he knew.
And he said to The Trake,
you could barely hear him,
"One with."
And the old man looked at Gil Hodges,
and nodded softly,
and looked over his loaves,
and felt them with his hands as if he were blind.
He chose the very best crusty one,
slit it open with a long bread knife
with a fork on the end he used to spear
three, all beef, kosher, best you ever had in your life
franks right off the grill,
anointed with a thick ribbon
of mustard from a cloudy squeeze bottle,
slathered with warm kraut,
tucked into that fresh crusty roll,
into a little white napkin,
and he handed it to Gil Hodges.
And Gil Hodges turned around,
crouched like Campy did,

and gave it to me.
He knew. And I knew,
what it said up on the wall at Gil Hodges Field is true -
"Man stands tallest when he stoops to help a boy."

He wasn't a dodger, at all.
He was a giant.
And I dream of Jack Kerouac,
in a little white hat,
holding out his hand
at Lafayette Coney Island -
when the world was as simple, and as composed
as a hot dog on a bun, with mustard, chili, and onions.

II.

Michael Rothenberg

We Turned the Universe

We turned
      the universe,
stars,
            pots and pans,
planets,
        piggy banks,
                comets,
cradles,
houses,
         suns,
             ponds,
pools,
   schools,
              libraries,
        bee hives,
              black holes,
    galaxies,
milky ways,
moons,
         storage rooms,

    asteroids,

    aquariums,

                briskets,

baskets

        cirrus, nimbus, stratus clouds

            and all the worlds

                  in general

upside down

                And now

        we are

                in deep

                      shit.

Eugene Stelzig

Things Unthinkable

When suddenly the unexpected and unthinkable
occurs, things appear in an entirely different
light. What was once invisible can now be seen,
what was once taboo can now be spoken
and heard by all, what was once utterly
beyond the pale is now the new du jour.
The shape of things has completely
changed at one fell swoop. The hidden
is here and now, said out loud without
any pretense of reserve. Soon the new
order of the day will be so routine that
once again it will be unheard and unseen.
The familiar world is still there in vestigial form,
but nothing will ever be the same again.

Dee Cohen

Wolves

The man who watched me skip rope
in front of my grandmother's apartment building.
The man who followed me home from school.
The man who waited at the corner in a paneled station wagon.
The man in the lobby of the dentist's office.
The salesman in the toy department of Macy's.
My uncle. My neighbor's uncle.
Uncles.
The man who rang the doorbell when I was home alone.
The man whose children I babysat.
My boyfriend's father.
My best friend's brother.
The man who drove slowly next to me
as I walked on Plainview Road.
Lots of men in movie theaters.
The man who caught the beach ball at the community pool.
The man who called 20 times in a row.
The man behind the bleachers.
The man who gave me a lift at the mall.
The high school custodian.
Dozens of men in the New York subway system.
A professor. A cab driver.
A tow truck driver. A cop.
The man who flew by me on a bike in a dim parking structure,
Lifted his head to the stucco ceiling, and howled.

Scott Wiggerman

Aftershocks

a golden shovel including a Dickinson last line (#799)

From some dark cavity, an affliction,
long-brooding, surfaces across America. It feels
like a brass-knuckled fist. What was impalpable

and buried has flared up and spread until
the ache of anguish is unbearable—ourselves,
our loved ones, in shrink-wrapped panic. How are
we to rise from chaos once unleashed and struck?

Gretchen Schulz

deluge

I

number one has already   rolled
overhead   number two is here
pounding on the door   number three
is on the way and should be arriving
in twenty-five minutes   four   five
six   and seven will be performing
by suppertime   please be seated
as the baritones and blowhards
the bass drums and windbags
the braggadocios   blast
this country   wide open

II

white out   freezes everything
in its path   the truth becomes
inadvisable   the known
is gone   the unknown   arrived
eyes close to harm   the damage
is drastic   mighty element
of greed is blasting through   it will
be the undoing of all strides
made forward   with winds blowing
tidal waves   crashing   copious
amounts of trash   all along
the shores of her beautiful self
where the vulnerable   sit naked
strangers   in a new country
light is barely visible
on the waters of lady liberty

Patrick Colm Hogan

from Travels in the Land of Pious Men
    (Written in July 2016, following the Republican National Convention)

At night, in dreams,
Choruses of demons
Scream into my ears

That the armies of the pure
Despise what we have done
And been.

When I wake up,
The angels of the One True God
Are dancing on my fingertips;

When I reach out,
My hands convulse
With violent quakes.

I cannot walk—
or eat.
Food spills off my plate.

Stray dogs lap it up;
I grow weak from hunger
And dismay.

From beneath the skin
My ribs shadow out and in
Their frail ridges.

When the disease strikes
You can never again
Retrieve the right word

Or hold a thought in mind
As long as the span
Of a hand.

When that time comes, who will tell
The enemy of the people
From the friend?

Jared Smith

Something Dark Beyond Words

There is something waiting in the autumn woods
there ahead right there beyond that crest that hollow
where shadows blend its red claws into the leaves.
You can smell it…something musky on the air
and it beats its massive paws up and down, a trumpeting
and tramping wholly out of place along this casual path,
but it waits for no one and it waits for anyone and
its roaring shakes the earth beneath your feet
and its drumming haunts the dreams of better men
and its drumming wakes its neighbors who start to sing
and they sing of blood and feathers and they sing
of armies trudging forward and they sing of earth
claiming what the seasons bring it out of time
and it's right there up ahead where the crest is
and you can smell it in the air and taste it on your tongue
and revulsion comes to claim you, pulls you back
from that path along the river where the leaves are turning
colors and you shrink into the shadows but it drags you
from your soul and it pulls out all your words and drips
them in the river scattered by the seasons and you
wish for better men and better women but they cry
and run when they see you on that path by the river
there is something in the woods and it is coming it is
no longer waiting in the pages of past history it is
darkness for the country and will burn out our tomorrows
and we have no trumpet to blow down its walls and fences
that were whispers in the wind not so very long ago.

John Berry

The Day Before It's Official

I saw a few squirrels today
a flock of wild turkeys
several species of songbirds
and a hawk

They appeared more twitchy more skittish
less peaceful than usual
and I would have blamed the hawk
but he too danced on his branch
fidgeting in his feathers

And then I thought about monkeys
in their iron cages
lions and elephants
locked in pitifully small savannahs

I wondered if the zebras shied
and the antelopes shivered
if the foxes
out in this field
slept uneasily in their dens

I wondered if the sharks in their twilit zones
at the Baltimore Aquarium
swam in lust or fear
their gaping mouths and razor teeth
quivering
eyes wide open like housecats watching
fragile wrens through a window

G.L. Brower

Autumn in the Bosque, Winter in America (2016)

And now it's winter
Winter in America
Yes and all of the healers have been killed
Or been betrayed.
But the people know, the people know
It's winter
Winter in America
……..
The Constitution struggled but died in vain
& now Democracy is ragtime on the corner,
Hoping for some rain
……..
The people know it's winter,
Winter in America.
—Gil-Scott Heron.

I

When cold seals the fate
of chlorophyll,
bosque cottonwoods fade to blonde
then curl brittle brown:

Yellow meanders north to south
from one cottonwood leaf
to another
through the valley,
as far as the eye can see
with jaundiced sight.

Leaves glide away
into the World of Wind,
or fall into an amber quilt
upon the river.

This change of leaf-life
arrives on a blanket of cold
that descends from Taos toward
Truth or Consequences of winter onset,
a saffron, arboreal river-trail.

II

The Rio Grande
thirsts from water depletion,
sandbars in its throat.

In the autumn of our discord,
a Big Freeze has brought
Winter to the Empire.

The first snow
of our Decline
is on the horizon,
roads filled
with dead snowplows.

III

Winter darkness extends
into all hours of the Future.

At home by the fireplace,
I listen to Debussy's *Clair de lune*,
look out the window toward the river
as flakes like crystal leaves
from the Tree of Storms
surge across a giant moon.

If each snowflake is a note,
blizzards are scattered symphonies.

Empires have been lost in this music.

Randy Prus

The Potomac by Moonlight

By the river,
lay your body down.
Skip stones across
the water top, until
they disappear
into silence.

Jim Cohn

Cold Moon

Cold Moon, I mourn for America.
I am in mourning for the world beneath sky.
Unwavering is yr devotion to practice.
You take in humiliation, fear, desire, uncertainty,
Yet give out nothing, nothing but light.
Many people come to you for emotional advice.
You set up a little table and chairs.
Most of your sessions last around 5 minutes.
All kinds of questions about all kinds of things.
How a mushroom discovers the forest.
How to take everything you feel & fight for it.
Cold Moon, you turn the wheel and futures change.
"Accept it or not," you tell a reporter.
"It's going to happen," you tell the policeman.

14 December 2016

Colleen Powderly

Grief: November 9, 2016

This line of larches stretches out forever
and I follow it. White pines on either side
thin and the ground rattles with slippery leaves,
dry and deadened, lifting to attempt escape
in the light breeze. I am led past
a burnt oak, lightning-damaged, hollowed
in the middle so it forms a place to hide.
Something lives there. I walk quietly.

My foot slips on flimsy leaves
and I lose hold, skid head first down
a hill and over an edge. I fall
through thick air, wanting it to clear.

But I find no clearing.
There is never a clearing.
There is only waking

among tall mushrooms, white, so pregnant
with beauty I know they're poison. I want to sit
beneath the tallest one, my back straight against
its smooth trunk, and pick pieces from its gills.
I want to eat them, will their tasty sweetness
behind my tongue, feel them crumble bit by bit,
slide down and down and down,
until they stop my heart.

Fred Whitehead

Remorse

This is a word that had fallen out of use lately
Proclaimed John Wayne:
"Never explain, never apologize"

But soon there will be a new kind of apology

For then there will be not only buyer's remorse
There will be seller's remorse at the same time
Because you sold your own soul
to the Devil
inside
Yourself

Next comes Expiation

Jim Cohn

This Week

Walking in moonlight,
I stepped in a big pile of dogshit.
The day before an arctic storm blew in,
My winter jacket zipper broke.
A therapist emailed me
To say he was very worried about
The state of my mind.
I should come in and talk.

I spilled a cup of coffee
On the modem & it fried.
A letter arrives to say the airbag is defective.
If activated, it may kill the passenger
It was installed to protect.
And then there's the inauguration,
The Inauguration of the Anti-Dawn,
With its voice of money & eyes of grope.

They say Love equals Hope
Outweighing Experience, but
Rose bushes do not turn into houses,
Rain does not make a door.
Sometimes a people walk barefoot
Without any coat into a blinding storm.
This is what is known in heaven as
"Magician entering the battlefield."

11 December 2016

Terez Peipins

As a Trumpet Warns

As an icy path leads
from your door,
one misstep
and you're down.
As a cancer diagnosis
given by a stern man,
threatens death.
As Earth's axis spins loose,
and this man
runs my country,
I shake my head
in disbelief.

John Roche

A Funeral Procession on Pennsylvania Avenue (January 20, 2017)
　　(incorporating some lines from Eric Bogle's "No Man's Land")

Roll out the caissons
Roll out the horse-drawn hearse
Lead out the riderless horse

Let us hear the 21-gun salute
Let us hear the answering howitzers
Beat the drums slowly
Play the fife lowly
Sound the death march as they lower us down
Let the band play the *Old Post* and chorus
Let the fifes play *The Flowers of the Forest**

For George Washington is dead
Thomas Jefferson is dead
Old Tom Paine is dead
Benedict Arnold is President

For Abe Lincoln is dead
Frederick Douglass and Susan B. Anthony are dead
Walt Whitman is dead
John C. Calhoun is President

For Teddy Roosevelt's dead
Gene Debs and Mother Jones are dead
FDR is dead
George Lincoln Rockwell is President

For John Kennedy is dead
Martin and Bobby are dead
Caesar Chavez is dead
The Grand Wizard of the Ku Klux Klan is President

For all the champions of liberty are dead
The Usurper assumes his throne
Mounts his own grand monument
Flanked by a mob boss to his left
And a foreign despot to his right

Ezra E. Lipschitz

Eulogy

It was a good country,
as national experiments go.
And many of its better citizens
will miss it terribly—especially
here around the holidays, a time
of year that its department stores
and online retailers loved so much.

But, decades of having our cake
and eating all of it too, led to a lot
of extra pounds and clogged arteries.

Diabetes slowly destroyed eyesight,
while causing severe nerve damage.

High blood pressure had us on edge
all the time and forced us to reduce
the salt of the earth in our diet.

In the end, it was all too much
and way too late. To the point
that the rest of the nations
averted their eyes when they
saw us cry on our death bed
through the closed window
of their television sets.

III.

Mary Dudley

How We Got Here

Smug, complacent,
we assumed superiority
and missed the fact that half
the people mightily were pissed

and they don't give a shit
about what we cared about
plus there were more of them
in states with college votes,
the ones that mattered in the end.

He won.

And, gloating now,
his orange face and hair shock us less
than the ideas he sends out.
Tweeting like a bird, he is.
Could never fly
but that doesn't matter.

What matters now
is how we stay together,
keep the planet safe,
and connect with those
felt sneered at and ignored.

Jack Bradigan Spula

Ballad of the Ballots

Oh where are the snow-jobs
Of yesterquadrennium
The names we wrote in
When the dry rotted dugout of state
Left us scraped and sinking
Puffing on a great barrier reefer
Alienated dead-ended but still
Advancing fantastical candidacies
With a flourish of the pen
at the sub-basement of the ballot:
Attila Alaric the Great Khan
Mickey Mouse Daffy Duck
Goofy Porky Pig Roadrunner
Humpty Dumpty all the better
To lead all the king's men
Against the imperative imperator
Dump the Hump and
The prickliest pick the
One and only Tricky Dick

And now the joke's on us
And His name shall be call-ed
Trump the Magnificent
From this day forward
The write-in jape ready for
Distant future exercises in democracy
Should there be any.

You won, we get it
But how you stole it
Fair and square
We don't quite get and yet
We're waking up to the
Sheer sheerness of it:
The clarity of an atoll lagoon
Where a dry-rotted
Dugout of State dropped us
On a sea-seething reef with waters
Warming and climbing to our knees

We know we didn't do enough
Or prosecute what was needed
To steer clear of the Colossal Wreck
Who sits golden in the Great Tower.
And oh the streets seem so far off.
But we will be in them.
Colossi have a way of crumbling
And down by the seaside
They make the kind of Big Splash
Nobody saw coming.
What more to say? Everybody
Into the pool.

Steve Coffman

Making Our Move

We did it, actually did it –
shot ourselves in the head!

Luckily in the glass half-empty part
long shriveled from disuse

Like my dear departed mama said
it's not wasted if you use it

So, save your sorrow for tomorrow
you're still alive until you're dead

Instead of pouting in your bed
learn to dance to that rattling lead

Jump to your feet, shout huzzah
shake it and bake it, cha-cha-cha

Shuffle your feet, wriggle your rump
bounce to the rhythm trapped in your bean

Or follow the beat of those camouflaged boots
Ka-trump Ka-trump, Ka-trump, Ka-trump!

11/9/16

Steve Ausherman

We Bind Our Own Feet

The teeth of the animal we have become are bared.
The long voter lines are silent and tense.
We are the vulnerable leg now hamstrung and bloody.
We have chewed off our own limb to escape.
The trap is of our own design; steel forged and angry.
We bite, bleed, struggle and succumb.
We thrash about.
We find no answers.
When the beast of the people is angry, blood will always flow.
We vote and we are angry. We no longer read history books.
We blind ourselves. We bind our feet.
We are nailed to a cross of our own making.
We chew off our own legs.
We forget that we still need to walk forward.
We have lost our strength to bear burdens.
To discern. To bear witness. To know.
We forget what it is to stand tall.
We forget what it takes to reach out a hand.

Patricia Roth Schwartz

Know Better

1

The way things end is often slow, each step
creeping up surreptitiously, a stealthy
yet ravenous cat, almost ignored, named
something else, even though we knew better.

2

Families in darkly furnished rooms, up late,
small glasses of amber drained, voices low,
talking talking, leaning close, re-naming,
calculating: it won't, he can't, we can't, let us
wait it out. Should have known better.

3

The flower of light that blossomed over
the sleeping city that devoured everything,
leaving only ashen shadows of what
had been mothers, workers, babies,
was years coming to fruition in bunkers
where white men scribbled on chalkboards,
smoking, knowing better.

4

Only the flimsy barrier of a door before
which bruised knuckles hang raised
stands between later and now.
There is no later. You hear your name.

What did you know?

Lalita Pandit Hogan

Of Blue

It was endless
Sky was, and sea
It was the future

The red, they thought was sun
Setting
Till it spread, all night
No one came out and said
Out loud: it is death
Coming to us, they felt its coldness
A face, rising behind another face
Reminded some of Arthur Miller's
Crucible judges. Some asked,
Arthur Miller? Who?

Blue, then, was no longer
The thing with feathers.
It was not the gentle blue jay
Of Wisconsin woods.

Numbers with curved feet
Jumped out of computer screens
Sneaked into
Fretful sleep ....
Morning brought certainty
A nightmare had begun.
No one could sleep anymore.

Torn feathers fly in the wind
Bird cadavers litter every
Niche. Apostasy needs dissection
Who is an apostate; who violated
A sacred shrine?

David Morse

Splitting a Crow's Tongue

Boys in my father's day claimed if you split
a crow's tongue, you could teach it to talk.

I imagine two or three boys:
one to hold the struggling bird while it shrieked,
another to grasp the tongue, and a third
to split it with a pocket-knife.

Did they actually go to such cruel lengths?
Maybe it was only a folktale passed
from father to son. But I know boys did
prove their budding manhood with feats
contrived to flummox grownups,
filling a belfry with pumpkins in the dead
of night, or taking apart a neighbor's car
and reassembling it astraddle a roof peak.

Today they hack into computer networks, run
for President on a platform of racism and lies,
split a whole nation down the middle
just to prove the crow can speak.

Larry Goodell

Us is U.S.

Oh fine time
of fine froth and time
the disgusting spray of madness
not from dog but from human
the madness of ignorance
frothing at the stupid words
of unthinking thinking
logic torn apart by
non-working cells
spit-out of repeated hearing
over the airwaves let loose from the net
the echoing of emptiness
of any fabric of sense
hate the cocoon of hate
flying from minds that make
no connection
to *any* compassionate sense
any love of the same exact
species as *any* beings of color
are despised as discolor
as Aryan madness bursts from
their pimple heads
and their mouths can't even mouthe
their lack of sense
covered with their flag of hope
they're the only ones worth living on the planet
as dumb lies make up their fragility

"I *shout* don't *speak* what my putrid mind
doesn't connect to my mouth"

hate is the *pure* race the fear of minorities
becoming majorities   deplorable   pathetic
screaming   maniacal   nonsense
gunning out their wild west protecting power
of their wealthy overloads
the super-rich they love to ignite them
they are the bombs of their hearts
exploding in love of shouting down

"We're in this together to boot us up
the ass of this country
aligned to the power gluts of the rich
we suck ass all the way as the ass and mouth
are the same in our narrow dream
what did you say, forward
is backward all the way
I'll blow you away with
my arsenal of white insanity
dumb to the point of
blithering nonsense
enter me in the dunce arena
I *love* to make you fear the day
you dared be different
thinking is dead as compassion of
creative instincts are non-words
as I eat up the earth and channel it
with my hate which is love for my
savior. Madness is
a frothing mouth delight don't you think
don't you think?
Join the club that's beating
everyone else down
to the ground. Only us is
U.S.
Stagnant stinking
us."

Holly Wilson

All Umped Up and Nowhere to Go

Frankly, I'm still completely stumped
By how so many people can be fooled
By well-choreographed hollow promises
Doled out by an egomaniacal chump

I don't want to be a grump,
But there's a lump in my throat
As I contemplate what may be coming

I can still feel the sting
Of the hard thump
On my progressive, liberal rump
From the vitriolic diatribe
Whipped up by a sociopathic strumpet

Are we about to dump all the progress
That's been made in one big clump?

No, I'm not all pumped up by the prospective
Of reversing the positive oversights we've achieved
While rich men and corporations get plump

Is it time to jump across the border to escape from a disaster,
Or should I stay and suffer the lumps of a political beating?

Is this country going to fall into a permanent slump,
Or is this just a temporary bump in the road?

Can freedom and equality win this high-stakes game,
Or is Vladimir holding all the Trumps?

Gayle Lauradunn

Tribal Shorts

"Go high" Michelle says "Go high."
She's had a lot of practice
being black, being woman.
The rest of us will have to learn.

    The doctor asked if I was
    feeling depressed.
    Oh, no, I'm joyful the water
    will be diseased
    the national parks will cease
    to exist, medical care
    a thing of the past. Shall
    I go on? Oil spills will occur
    in every ocean without penalty.
    No, I'm not depressed. Just
    wish I lived another time another place.

        Last year in Norway the woman
        who has lived seventy years
        in a tiny village on the Sognefjord
        asked why those people hate Obama.
        They are Republicans, I said.
        She nodded pensively. They
        certainly are, she said.

Kathamann

Maybe This Is Why

My sisters are grandparents now.
Another generation being imprinted
with the same ethos as we were.

Living in a Rusty State of
penny-pitching, coupon-swapping
parties, shopping secondhand. Their
high school mentalities have gotten
them this far.

That's all the further they wanted to
travel. Remain the same.

Changes were too much for them.
They were already buckled down
for the duration.

They never vote.

Joe Weil

Red State Polka

I see red everywhere, though I'm losing my hair,
and I hate it, it's boring and sad
where the fair becomes foul and the foul becomes fair
and a nation goes stark raving mad.
It's red in all branches, the rich on their ranches
are branding, and Godly, and charmed
and pretending to be, just plain folks, don't you see,
they're the salt of the earth? (and well armed)...
Burn all the books, save the guns, and the looks
of the women. As trophies they count.
All the girls must line up from the A to D cup
to see if they're worthy to mount.
Oh give me a home where the buffalo roam
past the frackers, and hackers, and hacks,
and no matter who's in-- his executive's grin
will fall upon old Goldman Sachs.
Yes the God-fearing bankers shall suffer no cankers
from mixing with greenbacks and gays.
And the Christian shall wave in the home of the brave
as he sings to his lord all due praise.
But if this is so, this sick medicine show
this conning, this lying, this spew,
then I'd rather be dead in the land of all red
where only God's heaven is blue.

Randy Prus

Red State Blues

I confess:
I don't know
these people
any more. I know
their habits of style,
habits of mind, but
am shocked by the habit
I do.

We've talked and walked
in the coolness of an evening
beneath a torrential July
Oklahoma sun setting somewhere
elsewhere.

Mornings, I walk the dog,
the moon & hope appears in the west,
disturbing the sleep of dreams,
the dying account of it.

It's the living in foreign parts
that will take us to home, to elsewhere.

Sylvia Ramos Cruz

Post-outrage

Post-truth was named Oxford Dictionary's
2016 word of the year, marking the place
we landed sliding down the slippery-slope
from Merriam-Webster's 2006 *truthiness*.

As I understand this new word,
in this new world
truth is a matter of belief.
Climate change is a Chinese hoax!

I propose another new word
for this new world, *post-outrage*—
the place we landed on 11/8
pushed off the cliff of the 2016 election.

The place where people, outraged over and over
by the man's words on women, Muslims, Mexicans,
guns in schools, nuclear weapons and just what is America,
find themselves— without an ounce of outrage left,
no matter what he does as president.
They're at *post-outrage*.

They don't understand how so many people listened
month after month, nodding their heads, maybe thinking
his words hyperbole— a way to shake things up—
or how those same people rejoiced
to see political correctness chased out the door.
Lock her up!

Perhaps the nodding people didn't know
he is a *post-truth* man who manipulates beliefs
rooted in everyday resentments about the changing color
of the world, lost privilege, shifting fortunes,
and a barely nascent 237-year-old nation in decline.
(Never mind the facts or figures!)

Perhaps they didn't believe this man knows
just where to grab the *post-truth* world
to get what he feels entitled to. And perhaps,
just perhaps, when their favorite ox is gored, sacrificed

at the feet of campaign promises, they'll feel outrage,
demand a better deal.

There is no better deal. We're in a new world,
post-outrage, for as Maya Angelou said,
"When someone shows you who they are,
believe them; the first time."

****

Post-truth: 2016 Oxford Dictionary's word of the year- circumstances in which objective facts are less influential in shaping public opinion than appeals to emotion and personal belief.

Truthiness: 2006 Merriam-Webster's word of the year- the quality of preferring concepts or facts one wishes to be true, rather than concepts or facts known to be true.

Ceinwen E. C. Haydon

And

And every time I said it cannot be it was
And this year's tides swept away the best
And our paltry attempts to swerve from cruel chaos
And our selfish hopes that we would stay untouched
And our shock at Jo Cox's slaughter
And our dismayed hearts when Europe drifted out of reach
And our helpless horror as children die in Syria, Yemen, in multitudes
in many places
And all the lies from newsprint, sound bites, misbegotten phrases
And all the divisions and differences that crystallised
And all our fear of stateless and abandoned people and backpacks
And our politicians' tough talk of hard boundaries and strict controls
And despair that leads to hate and fear that leads to hate and
fear that leads
And who knows what gross attacks on either side of damned divides
And then the Arctic ice cap melts with unprecedented speed and swells
the oceans
And undertow of manmade tides and storms that tug our world
towards destruction
And in America the forgotten ones raise a scream ferocious
with demands
And Trump arrives, Mr. President, man-toddler with his finger
on the button.

Dennis Maloney

from The Faces of Guan Yin
(a work in progress)

Darkness descends
on the empire
as the old men try
to reassert their power,
embrace the twins of
ignorance and arrogance,
and find the key to reopen
the half-buried trunks
of hate and bigotry.

We see them use
language to manipulate,
distort, deny, and betray
the reality of facts.

The smell of despair
is in the air and fear
of the other reemerges.
The silent rage
before the judge
renders his verdict
that there was no
terrorist among us.

Can we ever reclaim
the power of language?
Our eyes filled with tears,
do you hear us knocking?

IV.

Jules Nyquist

Zozobra and the Hallelujah Chorus

O Praise Him! The choir sings
Cruel and mighty rise up in merry
America elects a new leader
        an outsider with orange hair
Glory in the highest praise
all we like sheep follow
        waiting for a savior

Be not afraid,
Cast your worries on Old Man Gloom
Pile your fears on Zozobra
He's coming to shake it up
Coming to set the leaders on fire
Strike a match to your papers
Add them to the bonfire

Zozobra walks right up to the White House
Kicks the money changers out
And suddenly there he was with the angel
He bears our griefs
Burns our sorrows
Black smoke rises, engulfs us all
Reduces everything to coals and ashes

Rise, flames, rise
The year burning
Why do the nations furiously rage together
Let us break their bonds asunder
Zozobra, heavy with our weight,
        breaks them with a rod of iron
With fire and trumpet sounds
Ashes, ashes, all will burn
Explode, volcanoes erupt with lava
Earth breaks open to swallow them all
Hallelujah!

Jack Hirschman

The Ashes of Nada Arcane

1.

In contrumpdiction
to states of things natural
and snatchural;

in canttrampdickshun
to whorveryone suffering
the demonizing

of Elgeebeetee;
in countertrumpery we
take this stand for

one and all against the fa,
against the far, against the
fart Right which, peturd

on peturd, day by day
and nightie by nightie
is soiling all the

boxers and punties
in this etherwise hopey-
get-lucky world.

2.

Seams that every
land which a decade ago
held a Left aloft

have split, what with
ignorance and pignorance
afoot, and now sing

the Internetionale
while Goldman sucks swallows
all the bluejawb sperm

of the banks and their
sementic essence which is
dough to make more bread.

In short, everybody's
being had, and knows he or
she is it, spelled shit,

who's short for Shitler
making a comeback in the
mouth of Donald Duck

Trump (seeing as Walt,
not Whitman, was another
pro-Nazi puppet)

and, as you very well know,
the billionaire
imperialists

want nothing more
than to control your very
kaka as they're

preparing a most
fartissimo explosion
of the nuclear

bomb that will begin
the Third World War and the end
of life as you know it.

3.

Yes, that's what's lying
under the lies you're being
asked to buy into,

and it's all arranged
beforehand because, just as
WW2 was fought

to bring television
to the masses, and the war in
Vietnam was fought

to bring the microchip
into existence and change
communication

between human beings
forever, though at the cost
of memory and feeling,

that's why there's just life
with a robot around
the corner, and the threat

of a U.S. president
who can start WW3
with a racist mouth

that can gather all
the swastika lovers
in his sty and

promise to outsuicide
islamic martyrdom by
a blast so powerful

the eyes of Venus
will roll in disbelief
and all the suns will

start weeping in our
galaxy uncontrollably,
and when they stop

and behold all that
nothingness that had
been our world,

they'll try recalling
even a particle of life,
a vein of leaf,

a nanosecond
on a digital clock,
a street, an infant

but there'll be nothing,
nothing at all, not even
a tree of life,

nothing but the vision
of nothing at all, just a
shimmering from the

ashes of nada
picking up echoes and volume
till it's sounding thunderously:

What a tragic waste!
All these centuries of life!
Nothing but a tragic waste!

Michael Peters

Excerpts from "O Beautiful Death™; A Rage Device Index"

goldman sachs psycho HR jedi mind-trick
(how to rig the system)

        with an ideological persecution complex
        a mein kampf puffer fish ego
        werewolf commandoes
              live mas™
              live fearless™
              to taste the feeling™
              just do it™
        O motion detector
        O glowing serums
        O ordinary essence
        the digits of death
        (your own finger tips)
        dance bluntly on flat screens
        & the rostrum trumpets?
        apply terms and conditions
        a privacy policy notice
        to milk your aphids
        in the pop culture fungus garden
        & in the distractions
        in eden's preface
        in securities
        all buy-outs secured

        [wave hand from left to right before the visage]

        these are not the predators you're looking for

six things predators know
(how to see their trigger fingers as they would want to target you)

O demonology task force
there are snipers in the tower of babel

O freudian roadkill
increase your rep reach
with dual branding
from centuries of meditating
on how others see you

in the hand's distraction
all speed   is politics

don't look now, the moon's shitting balloons!
what was that? I don't know
better ask google

    siri,   how much is a hazmat suit?
    siri,   how much is a drone?

we can see you
& your little snowflake poem?
 it's about to implode

    into sea horse squadrons
    spewn from a pouch
    into jellyfish semen festivals
    from oral cavity to oral cavity

Oh grab a tentacle, any tentacle
hang on, ride the free market
to where all   bubbles
swell to rise

    upward

    upstate guns

"for all your shooting needs"

cosmic agoraphobic imploding stochasm detector in the identity sphere
(the iktomee fundamentalist weather report)

        god damn it, this empirical space helmet's all fog'd up
        dark energy
                information
        all about

        me

        like jesus
        in the bowels of the ronald reagan building

        but that's enough talk about me
        let's talk some more about   me
        O always me

        a hubble kinship
        to know
        magellanic clouds & dust
        can take new shapes

        "there you go again"

        but fashy, this time
        self-radicalized
        & saddled with a mea-psychosis

        stepping up into the stirrups of your *new* afterlife
                flying saucer
        alien goose-stepping michelangelos with reaching arms
        it's only a "roman salute"

        for mine is the kingdom

Rudy Rucker

The Third Bomb © *2006*

This piece was conveyed to me by my now-vanished friend Frank Shook. I published it under my own name in issue #2 of my zine Flurb, still online at www.flurb.net. 'The Third Bomb' appeared in 2006, at the nadir of the Bush-Cheney years. I take no responsibility for Mr Shook's incendiary political stance, nor do I vouch for the facts of his account. But his tale seems fitting for this slim 2017 volume Trumped, *published by the redoubtable John Roche in reaction to the advent of the Trumpic States of America.*

I'm imprisoned on a jungle island. I think it's in the Caribbean near South America. Can you hear me? I'm sending this out live on the Web by talking to myself under my breath so that it makes a slight hum or moan in my larynx. The sound resonates up my throat and into the SWN transmitter that Dr. Robards implanted it in my back tooth today.

SWN means Saucer Wisdom Network. Dr. Robards is the prison dentist. I've been live on the Web ever since the anesthetic wore off. My molar had an abscessed cavity; the man put in a large plastic filling with, I firmly believe, a transmitter inside. What makes me so sure? When I was leaving the office, Dr. Robards looked at me and made the Saucer Wisdom gesture, cupping his hand down and moving it rapidly to one side. I saw this very clearly.

But, yes, maybe prison life is getting to me. Maybe I'm going crazy, sitting in the corner of my cell crooning to myself and thinking I'm broadcasting. Radio Free Me. It's very stressful here, that's for sure. They pipe country music and political speeches into our cells, always with crackling static and unpredictable shifts of volume. It's been weeks since I had a good night's sleep. The ugly noise gets into my head, driving my thoughts.

There's a guy here from Quebec with a really strong voice. Jean-Claude. Sometimes he sings over the piped-in crud, bellowing "O Canada" or "La Marseillaise," temporarily drowning out the horrible music: the grainy-voiced alkies, the caterwauling prowler-gals, the warbling yearners, their witless rhymes like hammer-blows.

Right now, as I'm broadcasting this, it just so happens that we're hearing the voice of our President. He sounds angry, like he always does. I wish I could blow off his head a second time. Not that it would matter any more than it did the first time I did it. Earth's doomed to become an alien refueling station unless the people of the world rise up together. I'm calling for armed revolution. Moaning into my tooth.

My jailers are fellow Americans. Some of them wear military uniforms with no identifying insignia, other dress in chinos and white shirts. Most of the other prisoners here are foreign. All of us are suspected terrorists, none of us is going to get any kind of normal judicial process. It's terrible to see the United States from the outside like this. To a man, our captors are deeply imbued with the sense that they're right.

How did I end up here? I blew off the head of the President of the United States; it was a close-range double blast with a twelve gauge shotgun. I was working as a dog handler for a duck hunt on a Michigan estate belonging to one of the President's cronies. The Saucer Wisdom Network machinated for six years to embed me into this post so I could take my shot. But, sad to say, blowing off the President's head didn't make a damned bit of difference. He grew a new head right away, alien echinoderm that he is.

Now, in retrospect, I see that the Saucer Wisdom Network should have expected this outcome. Far from being paranoid and delusional, we in the SWN have been too conservative. The situation is worse than any of us had thought. Not only is Earth beleaguered by a race of alien sea cucumbers, but the President himself is a sea cucumber. He's working full time to foment nuclear war so as better to serve the Galactic Empire's UFOs.

The President's inner circle hushed up my assassination attempt. Harry Watson, the guy who owned the estate, certainly saw what went down, but right away one of the President's men gave Harry a light blast of buckshot to the face. The Secret Service took Harry to the hospital and loaded him up with those drugs that wipe out traumatic memories. Even if old Harry does remember anything, he'll damn straight know to keep his mouth shut.

There's so much that the public doesn't know. Thank Gaia I've got this subvocal laryngeal transmitter in my tooth. I've got nothing to lose by broadcasting the truth, that's for sure. I'm doomed.

The reason my jailers haven't executed me yet is because they're busy interrogating me. When my time's up, they'll stage my death as a suicide, like they always do. There's been three "suicides" on my cell-block since I arrived.

But it seems like there's some kind of gap in the chain of command. Rather than grilling me for information about the Saucer Wisdom Network, my interrogators are bent on getting me to confess to being an Islamic terrorist. Which makes me a round peg in a square hole. Terrorism is square; UFOs are round.

Agent Marc Walladi calls me in for debriefing every day. I keep telling him the truth about I why tried to kill the President: he's hell-bent on steering our planet into nuclear war. But Walladi acts like he thinks I'm either lying or crazy when I try to give him the deep background: about the third bomb and the fizzled tests and the sea cucumbers. On the other hand, maybe he's playing dumb to draw me out. Maybe, come to think of it, they deliberately put the transmitter into my tooth so I'd spill even more. Maybe my signals are going no place but to the titanium laptop on Agent Walladi's steel desk. I better not give out any details about the SWN's inner operations.

It's hot in this cell block, maybe a hundred degrees. We're all tense and sweaty. The hideous country music warbles on; the guards suffer from it too. A passing guard beats his club against the bars of my cage; he's yelling at me to stop moaning; he's calling me names. Idiot. I yell back at him.

"Storm trooper! Sold-out tool of the alien sea cucumbers!"

I go back to my tooth-moaning, but a little quieter than before. I definitely don't want the guard to come inside my cell.

Two cells down, Jean-Claude starts singing "Gens du Pays," a Quebec anthem. The guard goes to beat on Jean-Claude's bars instead of mine. So now I have a little peace again.

A German hippie girl named Ulrica told me about the third bomb a few years ago. Thing is, near the end of World War Two, the U. S. actually prepared three atomic bombs: one for Hiroshima, one for Nagasaki, and one for Berlin. The U. S. dropped the third bomb on Berlin after the blasts at Hiroshima and Nagasaki.

There are two seeming logical holes in the story: first of all, the U. S. would have had no legitimate motive for bombing Berlin, as by then Germany had already surrendered. Second of all, it's a matter of historical record that Berlin was not devastated by an atomic blast on August 11, 1945.

As for the motive — it's not hard to suppose that our leaders authorized the Berlin bombing for financial gain, as a power-game gambit, for revenge, or simply out of inertia. As for the lack of historical record — yes, the third bomb was ignited over Berlin, but a flying saucer swallowed up the blast.

Goddamit, here comes the guard again. I'm too excited, I'm moaning too loud. Maybe I can scare him off.

"Lickspittle lackey! Don't even think of coming in my cell! I'll rip your face off."

Oh oh, he's getting out his keys. But, thank god, there goes Jean-Claude again, even louder than before. The guard roars back to Jean-Claude's cell, billy-club upraised.

Quickly now. Ulrica showed me a notarized translation of a report by a Berlin beer-garden waitress named Vilma Hertz. Shortly before noon on August 11, 1945, Hertz was on break, smoking a cigarette and staring up at the sky from the shade of a chestnut tree. A US B-29 Superfortress was droning high overhead. Hertz spotted a black object dropping from the plane. Just as she formed the thought that the object might be a bomb, it bloomed into a pinpoint of blazing light. But a moment after that, a silvery disk swept across the sky to envelop the burgeoning explosion.

Yes! A UFO ate the third bomb. The aliens were on the spot and ready for it; they'd been alerted by the Hiroshima and Nagasaki blasts of August 6 and 9. And why did the alien craft swallow the blast? Obviously they use nuclear blasts for fuel. Oh shit, the guard is back.

"Leave me alone, you monkey redneck! I'll moan all I want. You want me to throw my slops at you?"

Gaia help me, he's coming in. He's holding — are those pliers? He knows about my special tooth! Walladi doesn't like the information I'm sending out!

Listen fast now. UFOs are very commonly sighted near nuclear test sites. The army shot down a couple of the saucers, everyone knows that sea cucumber aliens are preserved in Area 51. Here's something new: the government hushes up the fact that most of the above-ground nuclear tests have been duds. The blasts were soaked up by the saucers, and that's why they went to underground tests.

"Get away from me, you filthy animal! I'll kill you!"

The UFOs want a regular series of blasts taking place in Earth's open air and that's why they want unending nuclear war. That's why we have a so-called war president in office! He's not a human being! He's an alien sea cucumber!

Oh no, here come the pliers! Rise up for peace, people of the earth! Rise up!

---End---

Tony Brown

Our Dragon

We claimed
we didn't know anything
about how this would be

right up to the day
the dragon we had been
feeding for ages

whose back had been
humping up the earth
like a monstrous gopher
for as long as we could recall

the one whose eyes like star sapphires
had dazzled us into long inaction
rose into full view

demanding our first-born,
our second-born, demanding to be
slaked and satisfied with our legacies

demanding everything
and nothing explicit because
his sheer sudden command
of the common sky

told us all we needed to know

We ran about like cinders
jerking crazily
in the general cloud of destruction

Becoming sparks that vanished
even as we flew
lost in the heat of a moment
we'd known was coming for years
and yet had denied
as easily as any other god
we'd ever taken on casual terms

Of course since we
had made this one ourselves

we still believed
we could remake it
right up to the second
that we fell consumed
back to the black ground

to enrich the soil for
whatever new folly
would follow

Kitty Jospé

No Trump
(Inspired by the play, "An Iliad", written by Lisa Peterson and Denis O'Hare)

Prélude,
And if there had been no contest, Paris would not have taken Helen,
and Menelaus would not have asked Agamemnon to get her back...
and the Greeks would not have captured the beautiful Trojan women,
and Apollo would not have shot them with plague-tipped arrows
and all that rage, boiling in the hearts of men could have turned to
passion for good...
but here we go, again : we sing of arms and men, *arma virum que cano*.

Again... the cards are dealt... spades promise graves,
hearts are denied, clubs go to work and promises glitter
in diamonds. We cry *3 No Trump!*
But the cards are dealt, words have gone awry
and rage is already blood-fire,
chasing good bye rational thought.

Cry out in Greek, cry out in dactyls, hexameters,
cry out thesis, arsis, however you name the parts;
Cano sings *no-no-no* but the arms and men
provide Trump
     to spear through another,
gouge out eyes, tie the tendons of ankles,
attach once-was noble heroes to wild-eyed
horses who will gallop for ten days, dragging
heads in the dust.
    There is no righteous war.

What is dealt in the name of *we will be great*
but trick after trick of unspoken fear. *Cano*
notes what is lost, hands down.

After battle, the shepherd, the farmer, the warrior,
the kings, on both sides, and the Gods sleep,
but we weep, for sons we held as infants,
  we weep, for friends with whom we laughed
    sob of arms and men unable to sing
      weep for what's lost
        weep...
          weep.

Bruce Bennett

Our Rough Beast
     (Updating W.B.Y.)

A sudden blow. The Great Mouth spewing still.
No one was ready for that Huge Defeat.
Now millions mourn, and there is crow to eat.
The Monster stalks. We take the bitter pill
And blame ourselves, the media, and those fools
Who loosed this Thing upon us. Couldn't they *see*?
Where were their minds? Their hearts? How could this be?
The fault's in everything: the polls, the schools,
The greed, the incapacity to tell
The difference between plain Truth and lies,
The eagerness to close one's ears and eyes,
Then damn one's enemies to Death and Hell,
All so a Cretin who can barely speak
Can hold us all in His indifferent beak!

Pris Campbell

Heading South

Polar caps float past the White House.
Men and women leap from the roof
onto rowboats, purloined sailboats,
documents about the myth
of global warning shredded quickly
despite Trump's objections.

I'll make America great again, he shouts.

Security Guards cling to the top
of the Empire State Building.
They wait for a large piece of debris
to float by before they jump,
hoping to cling, Titanic style,
until the lifeboats come back
to get them.

The Statue of Liberty sighs in sorrow,
takes a deep breath before the tides
overcome her.

At the docks, immigrants, already loaded
for deportation, let loose the dock lines,
pick up floating men and women of all colors,
the elderly, women from rape camps,
Gay couples separated, now united again,
the homeless, lost children.

They add poets and artists to document
this shifting New Age, head south
with a crude map to where word
has spread that Atlantis, long sunk,
has risen again just for this day in history.

Gregory L. Candela

Trumpet of God

Perfectly coiffed, thin, mustard, ski-jump hair
perfectly pursed lips and gleaming feral
teeth: your non politically-correct
notes, breaths, perfectly pitched riffs
in the jam of our uncivil discourse.

Trumpet of God, you evoke
passion from the mob: "You're Fired!"
In the slaughter, the burning, of sinners
primed for the flames, you blow
like Gabriel, the winds of rage.

Trumpet of God, we embrace you
Satchmo to our angry, wailing
toothless, stretched old mouths
media spewing in the face of hope.

Prophet, blow the loud jeremiad in
the desert of our desiccant hearts.

Trumpet of God.
Oh, how we all, every one,
on your right
on your left
deserves to be
in your small hands.

V.

Caitlin Gildrien

Transition

Remember the change in pitch
after your water broke,
when you could no longer tell
yourself that what you were feeling

was "an interesting sensation
requiring all your attention,"
when you could no longer tell
yourself you were feeling
anything but pain? Remember

how your voice dropped
low when the pains hit,
and how the midwife nodded
and murmured approvingly.

Now something was happening.
Remember how, then,
after a while,
the low moans pitched
upwards sometimes into
shrieks? You wanted something

different, a YouTube birth, the kind
you get when you type in "gentle
peaceful home birth" but
you were not at home
and you were, in the end,
screaming.

I think this is like that.
I think it's going to be.

We are in the low moans now.
The hope of a peaceful
revolution flew off with that sparrow
from the lectern,
and those still seeking revolution
do not seek peace.

Mostly these things
are bloody,
in any case.
Most often they make
a mess.

And now we're dilating,
we're breathing hard,
and we're going to have
to work now,
going to have to push,

even though we think it'll tear us in half.

It's months too late
now to change our minds;
the question now is whether,
and which of us,
will make it through alive.

Alan Kaufman
Let Us (For the Poets of January 15 and the Women of January 21ˢᵗ)

Let us
take ourselves aboard a bus
and travel to the dispossessed
and let us praise their dreamless eyes and hardened smiles
with rogue words of truth
in the killing fields of their hopes
the slum wards and ragged towns and stolen farms
Let us take to them the carnival of our mad and scattered lives
Let us bring them the mountain, let us give them the vision
of an open window, an unlocked door, a bed to sleep in, a plate of food
Let us give them the keys to the house of our love
Let us bare our throats tattooed with roses, our breasts sequined with
diamonds
our loins hot with dragons, our hands and feet pierced with beauty
Let us come to their dusty squares and drinking holes with canticles of
magnificent defeat
Let us deliver in their mangers of pollution and penitentiaries,
shopping malls and tenements
the hard, beautiful birth of the heart
Let us bring renewal
Let us declare the death of despondency and tyrants
For I have seen our campfires beside the roads like fallen, still-burning
miraculous stars
I have seen our bus voyaging to innocence
I have seen us tossed this century like a bone
after ninety years of science and war, reason and corporation
art and Auschwitz
I have seen my vocation descend like a pen to a page
that can never be filled with enough truth
I have crossed a continent of despair and I swear to you, Poets,
I live for greater than myself
You, street-Latin Elizabethan hustlers, I tell you time has come to deal
death's passionate kiss to kings
Time has come to bare our asses in Paradise
Time has come to write the Constitution with our poetry and flesh
Time has come to costume up for Liberty and ride
with words like steel-tipped whips
into the soul of America
and rage there and sing
till the mouth of every starving child
is fed

Gino Sky

Ommmmmm Mani Safety Pin Hummmmm
Buddhamas ~ 2016
(After The Election
At the Cowboy Buddha Hotel)

The gluten free cookies are Colorado high
Solar lights are needed now more than ever.
The Blue States have joined Brexit.
The Cuban Cigars were picked off at second base.
The Tao is spirit-wrestling the Dow Jones.
The NRA was gifted the rights to the Big Bang.

Tibetan monks are ooooooommmmmmming
their lower chakras off.
The New Testament is rewriting itself into *Hamilton* Rap.
The Great Mothers have cried for all the white women
who voted for the PG. (pussy grabber)
Fear of the new Supreme Court, Coyote & Road Runner
have upped their marriage date.

The Ghost Shirt People have been passing out peyote buttons
Like Crazy . . . (Horse).
Aunt Molly Jackson & Joe Hill have checked into the hotel.
The ACLU has taken over the honeymoon suite.

The safety pin is what's keeping us strong.

Ommmmmm mani safety pin hummmmmma

A. D. Winans

Trump Land

I cannot pledge allegiance to a racist
Who stands behind the flag
Whose principles you defile

I will not bow down to Corporate America
And its religious right

I cannot accept your moral bankruptcy
Your greenback God selling lives
On the stock market exchange

I will not bow down to a country where
Immigrants are treated like criminals
And women as chattel

A country whose papal church
Has its own bank where
Ka-ching ka-ching is the new holy mantra

America you have become
One big insane asylum
Your manic depressive innkeepers
Waging war on the masses

Your henchmen standing proud
On your purple majestic mountains
Kissing the cold stone faces on Mount Rushmore
Where you measure your inclusion
Looking like a Mafia Don with the
Cold kiss of death on your breath

Margaret Randall

Nothing at All to Learn

Original manuscript pages written
by the first woman to fly
or the idol who reveals affairs
we've known about for years
top Sotheby's sales this season:
readers eager for words
written with them in mind.

These are not broken wings
folded across breasts
that sorrow or burn
but maps inviting judgment
of those not yet here
who will wonder
at what we thought and did.

I too keep a journal I share
with family and friends.
I too write for posterity
—as the saying goes—
eager to leave an open window
on this life I inhabit,
what I see and feel and know.

But today I remember the diary
I kept as a teenager
traveling with my parents
to places they thought exotic:
"The waiter's nails were clean,"
I wrote after lunch in Rio:
young arrogance, sad legacy.

Sometimes the words that say the most
are those we would erase
from every memory,
disown from this old arrogance
where we pretend
we were born in perfect balance,
nothing at all to learn.

Michael C. Ford

Martyred Saints
                    (To/ the memory of John Cornford)

Cold black mountains of Fascism
Mounting towards the back of his
Skull and the swell of weapons was
A commitment wave to the wound
Which gave the grave to him as the
Orwellian prophecy advertised that
Death is what cannot be seen coming
Which is the way it was when all that
Republican resistance putting his 1936
Life on the line is wasted by bullets
delivered by Franco messengers and
Pumped into any poets defending the
Cordoba Plains in the same manner
Righteous writers are consumed in a
Homegrown womb provided by the
Absolute thrusting on of the birth of
A disparate complicity with soldiers
Intermittently injected with hot
Adrenalin of political blood and a
Cold aversion to corporate plasma

Kenneth Gurney

Blowing Steam 18 Dec 2016

Fuck Trump for his rating scale objectification of women.
Fuck Trump for his billionaire sense of privilege.
Fuck Trump for calling Mexicans rapists and drug dealers.
Fuck Trump for his inane but consequential bluster.
Praise Trump for defeating Ted Cruz.
Fuck Trump for suggesting Ted Cruz's father killed JFK.
Fuck Trump for his early morning tweet storms.
Fuck Trump for his blatant discrimination pandering.
Fuck Trump for his lowest common denominator campaign.
Fuck Trump for his berating gold star parents.
Fuck Trump for ridicule of the handicapped.
Fuck Trump for his seventy-five percent Politifact liar rating.
Praise Trump for hearing the struggling rustbelt workers.
Fuck Trump for his assaults on the first amendment.
Fuck Trump for his pandering to white supremacists.
Fuck Trump for his unpublished tax returns.
Fuck Trump for the malicious nickname labeling.
Praise Trump for sending Chris Christy out for Pizza & Oreos.
Fuck Trump for flouting campaign finance laws.
Fuck Trump for his bad hair.
Fuck the Christian Right for cozying up to a braggadocio sinner.
Fuck Trump for his non-stop finger pointing.
Fuck Trump for encouraging Brownshirt political violence.
Fuck Trump for his prominent fat-cat belly.
Fuck Trump for trafficking with Newt Gingrich.
Fuck Trump for encouraging Russian computer hacking.
Fuck Trump for belittling John McCain.
Fuck Trump for copyright violation music usage at campaign stops.

Fuck! Trump won!

Fuck Trump for saying he won the popular vote.
Fuck Trump for costing New York City millions to protect his fat ass.
Fuck Trump for charging the secret service for staying in his tower.
Fuck Trump for denying climate change.
Fuck Trump for his dangerous two-China bear poking.
Fuck Trump for his lack of security briefings.
Fuck Trump for thinking he is so damn smart.
Fuck Trump for placing too many generals in his cabinet.
Fuck Trump for placing too many wall streeters in his cabinet.

Fuck Trump for realizing Rick Perry's nose is the deepest brown.
Praise Trump for meeting with Romney and Gore.
Fuck Trump for regularly mangling the English language.
Fuck Trump for cozying up to Putin.
Fuck Trump for insider trading and stock manipulating.
Fuck Congress for allowing insider trading and stock manipulation.
Fuck Trump's kids for charging a million dollars for daddy access.
Fuck Trump for telling China they can keep the navy drone.
Fuck Trump for his big, beautiful border wall pipe-dream.

Larry Goodell

Buy Free Speech

"I don't know about 'free speech' maybe it's a good idea that we should have to pay for it. Maybe at $20/month for 2 hours of 'free speech' regulated of course. I mean if you want to say anything on your mind, especially anything critical that will pass our censor, that should be about $200 for 20 minutes. Register first at Speech Control, Inc. at Trump Towers. Registration is only $100. We have other offers too up to $20,000 for one full week of 'free speech' with only a minimum of controls. Contact Donald Jr, Tiffany, Eric or Barron."

The only alternative is at this link: https://www.freespeech.org/

Jim Fish

Election 2016

They got what they want
They have no excuse

We got what we deserve
We have no excuse

They got what they want
They took their idiocy
To its logical conclusion
They have no excuse

We got what we deserve
We have had our chances
We have wasted our chances
    Trying to appease them
        Trying to cooperate with them
        Trying to work within their broken system
        They have done nothing but obstruct
They have no excuse
We have no excuse

We got what we deserve
For failing to call their hand
For electing
Our own
Corrupt
And spineless politicians
We have no excuse

They have no excuse
We have no excuse

I suggest
We sit back and watch
Give them their two years

I suggest we do nothing
    But watch
        Obstruct as much as we can
        And work on the mid-terms

Dick Bakken

Star Spangle Banter
> *(Fourth in ongoing "Eddie the Fish" series of "Fish Wrap" poems)*

Eddie splashes dance he calls Go / Slop It Down Donald.
Trumpster hops to the right, / bops to the left, then he waffles.
I vanna Go! screams his sweetie / as she rocks in her bikini
while he beams out all TV / *Yo! no problem with my weenie!*

ah-boomba-shikki-*sham!* / a-boomba-shikki-*shoo!*
ah-boomba-shikki-*sham!* / a-boomba-shikki-*shoo!*
you-you-you oooh-ah slippery you
you-you-you *shoo*-ah lippy you

Eddie flicks the frilly fins / as Ivanna backflips in
somersaulting out her halter / like dolphins slapping water—
Trump crawls from our dumpster / so shook up to hook and hump her
to his squandered wall, hollers / she can hold all Mexi dollars.

ah-boomba-shikki-*sham!* / a-boomba-shikki-*shoo!*
ah-boomba-shikki-*sham!* / a-boomba-shikki-*shoo!*
you-you-you oooh-ah slippery you
you-you-you *shoo*-ah lippy you

Ocean's zillion dazzling fish / swish a finny flop and kiss.
As Trump gets bumped from Prez / Ivanna has long jumped the rez,
rolls sparkles into ocean / such color-bursting motion—
flashed Blackfish / Yellow Fin / Red Snapper / Flounder golden!

ah-boomba-shikki-*sham!* / a-boomba-shikki-*shoo!*
ah-boomba-shikki-*sham!* / a-boomba-shikki-*shoo!*

Everyone!
Dump Trump's Rump! Dump Trump's Rump! Dump Trump's Rump!

Steven Deridder

Supercharge

I.

I am pumped for Trump
to systematically breakdown
the budget
on cardboard— spin on his toupee
like a sprinkler for cash
to water his donors: growers of their own
American dream.

I am pumped for Trump's
inauguration speech
triumphantly given, and I am pumped
for the contradictions he'll make
the next day,
but *mostly*, I am super-pumped
to hear friends paraphrasing
what hoops his followers jumped through
to make their President make cents.

I am pumped for Russia to rush
a statement out in hours,
that says nothing.

I am pumped for narcissists everywhere
(who I anecdotally, shamelessly presume
make up about 40% of America)
to rise up against each other—
the militant liberals throwing their safe spaces
around the neck of sexism, giving their opposition
a good strangling that silences everyone
as Trump's pets rationalize
their habitual hate
with tweets like horns all playing one note
all day
and night
despite being blue-faced, unable to mouth-breathe,
for it doesn't take air to repost, re-share, re-say
what everyone else is feeling or thinking.
It doesn't even take a brain, or a body.

This, here, now— is a shout-out
to militant conservatives,
to keep the illusion of a balanced act
going.

Though the scales are weighted,
we are all adult individuals, here.
We put our coins in the jukebox.
We weed our own newsfeeds, just fine.
What did you want to hear?

"I am pumped for the future"?

It's gonna cost you.

II.

On the paper stage, I am pumped to see
not where this is going
but where I will end up, being both gay
and unable to repeat
what everyone else thinks
I should be feeling or thinking.

Off the paper stage, I am pumped for nothing.
I am silent.
I am waiting for someone with power
to grow up.
I am waiting for the friends who never text.
I am waiting for America to be sold to China.
I am sifting through the media, searching for the news.
I am waiting for my phone to recharge
so I can write more, and text an America
in my head
that doesn't exist.

I would be pumped to guard what I love
with a gun, but I got caught smoking weed
in New York, once.

I would use my camera to fight,
but the pictures I take
don't get any likes.
They aren't pretty.

Thus, I am pumped for the future to hurry up and get here
like an award ceremony in which everyone gets
their own shining star, unique like a snowflake,
and forgets what's happened,
and checks their texts...

Bill Nevins

Fascist Religions Make You Feel So GOOD

"White people say the cutest things."—Danny Solis, spoken in the Golden West restroom, circa 1999, during the Poetry and Whiskey sessions

So why don't the Rolling Stones sue Trump's candy-ass for expropriating their best songs to blast over the speakers at his Mussolini Lite rallies, like the one in Burque the other night?

Time is On My Side
You Can't Always Get What You Want
Let's Spend the Night Together

Shit I found myself singing along with the Trump fans
while they jostled each other and gobbled processed cheese spread
and jalapeños on white corn chips

Decked out in their red and blue and white best
Bomb ISIS Build the Wall buttons
and appetites

Fuck, for a while I thought I was at the Celtic games, a football party or, shit, a Stones concert!

Neil Young

In Praise of Hecklers

Because someone's got to be the one
to lob bottles from the back of the stalls,
shout out "shit" when others rise
to cheer and call encore
and someone's got to refuse to fit
when others bite their tongues and conform
and dissent becomes the language
of consensus – it's the norm
and someone's got to say: "Fuck this!
Brand me. Ban me. Gag me. Censor.
Send your goons, your lackey-cops,
I'll take my bows as your tormentor."

Fred Whitehead

The Eighth of November

Remember, remember!
The eighth of November,
Republican treason and plot;
We know of no reason
Why Republican treason
Should ever be forgot!
Donald Trump and his crew
Did the scheme contrive,
To blow up the Dems and Hillary
All up alive.
Then at night the plot
They did hatch,
And proceeded
To strike the electoral match.
If you won't give us one
We'll take two,
The better for us,
And the worse for you.
A rope, a rope to hang the Clown,
A penn'orth of tacos to choke him,
A pint of piss to wash it all down,
And a jolly good fire to burn him.

Don Paul

We Hold the Cards for an Old and New Way

We're only human. We want to believe.
"The Donald" is real as poor folks' daytime dreaming.
Real as a threat. Real as a Christ (Father's middle name).
We want to have our hopes and fears palpable through One again,
Though one so in debt must be in part puppet,
His pride and insecurities
Making another perfect Devil's advocate.
You see, all of our Donald's big deals
Owe to creditors:
Lansky and Rothschild and Rockefeller
Back in the '80s,
Deutsche Bank, Goldman Sachs, and Bank of China now;
Resorts International in Atlantic City,
Towers in Manhattan, blocks in San Francisco.
Six times a bankrupt, our News-raised puppet
Stands and speaks at the will of those who hold its strings.
What, then, do they, the Ruling Few at the top of John's hill,
Want from their latest President salesman?
They want MORE of their usual, we may be sure.
MORE oil-and-gas profits, MORE of us digging deeper in mines and in Net,
MORE of us divided by races and classes unto blindness for War.
"Any War 'll do," the biggest gangsta Banksters
Crow from neon dawn till after midnight. "Any War 'll do"
for more debt.
What, however, if this card in their deck,
The Donald, our Donald, long-groomed as an Elvis or Beatle
Plays his own hand? What if he's different,
Different like Jackson, Lincoln and JFK
In refusing more Debt-from-Wars to feed Europeans' private Central Banks?
What—strange and yet common the contemplation!—
If our Donald becomes a true champion of the poor
Who elected him to serve their long-diminished desires?
What if our Donald grows noble as President of the United States?
His uncle John knew radar and Tesla's liberating work with energy.
What if our Donald chooses to step away from the C.I.A. U.S.A.
That's subverted freedoms with its brutal coups since before that Agency began?

We may hope. We may hope for such an improbable change.
We may hope that our Donald's drive to be HUGELY benevolent triumphs.
We, however, don't need to wait for change to be made good.
We're much MORE powerful than any head of State.
We're MORE than 71% of the potential U.S. electorate.
Also, we weigh the ox and count the jellybeans most correctly.
Our collective wisdom and compassion are greater than any One.
We hold the cards. The Ruling Few need us to use their Cards.
We know that we need water, not Wells Fargo, and we know
The old cycle that Citibank's boom must lead to more bust for us and bail-out for them.
Withhold our play with their cards, Wells Fargo, Citibank, Exxon Mobil
And any arm of all Cartels must fail.
So we can win. The Sioux and MORE at Standing Rock
Show us the way. Ojibwe in Wisconsin, Quinalt, Lummi, Yakima,
… in Washington,
Cities of Seattle, Minneapolis, … the Navaho nation, …
MORE than $28 in individual accounts divesting from Banks hat fund the Dakota Access Pipeline, …
Show us the way. Wind and sun can make more profits than oil and gas.
A new and old way opens as we start our 2017,
Old as Generosity, Courage, Fortitude, and Wisdom,
New as the devices that may connect Compassionate Action worldwide,
And so we can know jolts and caresses from Her above.

Joe Weil

Poem at Thanksgiving. 2016
    (To whoever kicked my pumpkin and wrote "Trump rules"
    on my sidewalk)

I sit down on my porch to play my flute
for the juncos
who are busy reaping the harvest
of pumpkin seeds splayed generously
across the snow yard by a wayward boot:

Thus thuggery has led to a "piping of plenty"
and I see the squirrels nibbling, too,
and no doubt deer, judging by the tattoos of their hooves
—each dye cast into the snow. Nothing at present moves
except my fingers along the flute's holes, the smell of the wood
where they were burned—still there,
at certain intervals, a whole note, each note
servant to the rest. I face the east where the hemlock
leans woozily and rocks above the neighbor's house.

Let the casual violence of someone's anger always lead me here:
Hardly any wind, my ass snowwet, but not painfully so,
my breathy blowing-- an amateur's song

against all that would swallow us whole, all that would
kick us dead. Let it be blessing, confounding
of the worst spirit-- bread.

Ed Sanders

Broom Poem

Bomb
then clean up

Strafe
then broom up

Laser
then swab up

Drone
then brush up

Hack
then pick up

The same
back to Pork Chop Hill

& then
all the way
back to Troy VIIA (1000 bc)

& beyond

Ed Sanders
What to Do?

It's not clear what to do
except to obey R. Crumb's
brilliant aphorism
"Keep on Truckin'"

If the military-intelligence establishment
in the 1960s, now long dead,
had not robo-killed JFK, MLK and RFK

United States history would have been much more peaceful
benign and sharing

So we're stuck in a vast predicament of
deliberate chaos and war

with an electoral system rife with cheating
and outright fraud

Many opinions on the Internet
urge us to "Rise Up" & defend
what's Good about the U.S.A.

& "defeat" the Bad

Except the Game may in effect
be Over.

And we poets, artists, musicians
& Bold Thinkers for an Egalitarian
Cradle-to-Grave Social Democracy
may just be yodeling in the
Canyon of the Abyss

and perhaps it's time to
examine Carefully
the Life of William Blake

for Clues on How to Live out our Decades
on this Border-bashing, war-maddened
Drone-batty, robotic battlement suffused
Situation and the Future it Seems to Foretell

Addenda.

Anti-Inaugural Masque
by John Roche
First Performance: *El Chante: Casa de Cultura*, Albuquerque
January 20, 2017

A play's the thing
E'en though no conscience hath this king!

Players:
The Raven Woman—Julie Brokken
The Chief Injustice—Bill Nevins
The Strumpet King—John Roche
The American Bard—Jules Nyquist
The Voice of the Ancient Barrio—Yasmeen Najmi
William Blake's "Voice of the Ancient Bard" read Liza Wolff Francis
Leader of the Chorus of Demos—Marcial Delgado
Drummer—Holly Wilson

Opening: As with W.B. Yeats' Noh-inspired plays (such as *At the Hawk's Well*), a masked figure (The Raven Woman), accompanied by ritual drumming, unrolls a batik cloth or flag banner or blanket that she places on the ground between the audience and the performance space, to mark a boundary, as it were.

The Chief Injustice:
By the Powers granted me by our honored Fabrication, and by the divine aroma of Moolah, and by the intercession of our atheist angel Ayn Rand,

I anoint you with this holy yellow water,
I anoint you with this oil of Exxon,
I anoint you with this balm of Billy Bob

And in the name of Reagan, the name of Nixon, the name of Bush the Elder and Bush the Younger, in the name of Merrill Lynch, in the name of Wells Fargo, in the name of Koch Bros., in the name of Philip Morris, in the name of the NRA, in the name of Breitbart and Fox, in the name of Putin, in the name of Beezelbub,

I crown you, Donald Littlehands Drumpf, the first Strumpet King of the United Stooges of AmeriKKK, and Vassel to the Holy Russian Petrostate.

Donald Littlehands Drumpf, repeat after me...
(Repeated by the Stumpet King):

I do solemnly swear that I will faithfully execute the Office of King of the United Stooges, and will to the best of my ability, preserve, protect and defend the Fabrication of the United Stooges and the Wishes of the Holy Russian Petrostate.

Now you may go forth to grope and plunder your subjects!

The Strumpet King:
Thank me all. Never seen such a Huuuge crowd, and such an assemblage of honored creditors. Joey No Socks, is that you on the bandstand? Wild! And we've got goodie bags for everybody: cufflinks and cologne and truffles and swag, you wouldn't believe it! And how about those Rockettes? All ten of them. And Russia, Russia, what can I say about Russia? Putin, who's a really nice man, a mensch, he sent the biggest most enormous bouquet to Drumpf Tower, so it's all good!

The American Bard:
Stop! Put down your vial of filth! Put down your book of blackest alchemy! Put down your Fabrication! I am the Bard of America Past. I speak the truths of Ralph and Henry, Walt and Woody, Emily and Red Emma, Langston and Ol' Doc Williams.

Put down put down your *magician's serpent, that all-devouring modern word, business.* Put down put down your falsities and obfuscations!
Put down put down your illusions of privilege!
Put down put down your racial animosities!

I speak for the Bards of Old, who knew, as did Merlin and Fergus and Taliesin, that a King without the Poet's Blessing is no King at all.

The Chorus of Demos:
Out, Demons, Out!
Out, Demons, Out!
Out, Demons, Out!
Out, Demons, Out!
Out, Demons, Out!
Out, Orange Diablo, Out!
Out, Orange Diablo, Out!
Out, Orange Diablo, Out!

Restore to us America
Restore to us Democracy
Restore to us our Better Angels
Restore to us the Rainbow
Restore to us Esperanza

The Voice of the Ancient Barrio:
I am the Voice of the Ancient Barrio, the Ancient Pueblo, the Longhouse, the Sky the Water the Land the People long before the highways the smokestacks the twisted laws and fabrications.

By the Powers vested in me by Turtle Woman, by Spider Woman, by the Sacred Mountain, by Gaia, by Demeter, by Loba, by La Llorona, by the Virgin of Guadalupe, by Purple Mountains Majesty, by the Ghost Dancers, by the Bison, by Standing Rock,

We Un-inaugurate you, Donald Puny Hands,
We strip you of all powers and potencies,
We repudiate your Fabrication, Chief Injustice,
We dissolve all your corporations
We discorporate all your Frankensteins
We return the dinosaur bones to the earth
And we dispel you, demons, to the place where nightmares go at dawn

The Chorus of Demos:
We deny you.
We defy you.
We delete you.
Out, Demons, Out!
Out, Demons, Out!
Out, Demons, Out!
Out, Demons, Out!
Out, Demons, Out!
Donald Puny Hands, you're FIRED!
You're FIRED!
You're Hell-FIRED!

William Blake, "The Voice of the Ancient Bard":

Youth of delight! come hither
And see the opening morn,
Image of Truth new-born.
Doubt is fled, and clouds of reason,
Dark disputes and artful teazing.
Folly is an endless maze;
Tangled roots perplex her ways;
How many have fallen there!
They stumble all night over bones of the dead;
And feel--they know not what but care;
And wish to lead others, when they should be led.

Closing: The Raven Woman, accompanied by ritual drumming, rolls up the cloth or blanket, and carries it out of the room.

Bios

Poems by **Mikki Aronoff** (10) also appear in *House of Cards: Ekphrastic Poetry*, *Rolling Sixes Sestinas*, *Snapdragon: A Journal of Art & Healing*, *Bearing the Mask: Southwestern Persona Poems*, *Value: Essays, Stories, & Poems by Women of a Certain Age*, *The Lake*, *3ElementsReview*, *Rat's Ass Review*, *Silver Birch Press*, *Legends & Monsters*, *EastLit*, and *Watermelon Isotope*.

Steve Ausherman (56) is a poet, painter and photographer who resides in New Mexico. He has been thrice nominated for the Pushcart Prize in poetry and has had two chapbooks of his poetry published entitled *Creek Bed Blue* and *Marking the Bend* (both from Encircle Publications).

Dick Bakken (103), born 1941, grew up in MT-WA-OR, but now since 1980 lives a mile high in Bisbee, AZ. Jump hard from his front porch and you'll land in Sonora, Mexico. *The Whiskey Epiphanies: Selected Poems 1963-2013* (www.pleasureboatstudio.com). *Pudding House #226 Greatest Hits 1967-2002* is now available only from dickbakken@yahoo.com

Megan Baldrige (18) is a retired English teacher, gardener, Japanophile, museum-docenting, garden-loving mom of four grown children, who has lived in Connecticut half her life, and Cedar Crest and Albuquerque the better half of her life.

Larry Belle (15) does not yet appear on the Professor Watchlist, considers himself a Sermon on the Mount social democrat and favors worker ownership and universal guaranteed income.

Bruce Bennett (88) is the author of the chapbook *The Donald Trump of the Republic* (FootHills, 2016), and now has more than enough Trump poems for a second chapbook, entitled *Our Rough Beast*. He is looking forward to his final Trump chapbook, *Requiem for a Nightmare*, which he hopes may be published within a year or two.

Currently working on his second volume of poetry, *Medicine*, **John Berry** (40) writes from his Winchester Va. home with his beloved wife, Brenda, and their constant yorkie companions, Molly and Lily. When not engaged in his profession as a woodworker and cabinet-maker, John hosts an internet poetry show, "The Sock Drawer Poetry Series," on www.winlifetv.com

G.L. Brower (41) has published six books of poetry and four CDs. He is the Editor of *Malpais Review*, a past director of the Duende Poetry Series of Placitas, NM, has taught at Kansas, UNM, USC, UCLA, UCSD, and in Spain and Mexico. He has also been a journalist (Spanish and English), and directed programs for Mexican migrant workers.

Tony Brown (85) is from Worcester MA. A six-time Pushcart Prize nominee, he fronts the poetry and music band The Duende Project. His latest chapbook is *In The Embers*, from Tired Hearts Press (2016).

The poems of **Pris Campbell** (89) have appeared in numerous journals and anthologies, including *PoetsArtists, Rusty Truck, Bicycle Review, Chiron Review, and Outlaw Poetry Network*. The Small Press has published six collections of her poetry and Clemson University Press a seventh one. A former Clinical Psychologist, sailor and bicyclist until sidelined by ME/CFS in 1990, she makes her home in Greater West Palm Beach.

Gregory L. Candela (90) has published scholarly articles in American literature, a volume of poetry (*Surfing New Mexico*—2001) and written seven produced plays. Recent publications include poems in *Circe's Lament, Malpaís Review, Adobe Walls, Sin Fronteras, Elbow Room, Monterey Poetry Review* and *Italian Americana*. Currently, he seeks a publisher for his poetry manuscript "Graveyards of New Mexico."

Steve Coffman (55) has taught writing at Michigan, Iowa, and Keuka College, and the Elmira Correctional Facility. In addition to fiction and memoirs, he has published two political essay/poetry collections, *Peace Meal* and *Messy Freedom*, and two poetry collections, *Off To A Bang: Poems of the New Millennium*, and *The Window*.

Dee Cohen (35) is a writer/photographer living in Albuquerque NM. She has published poems/stories/photos in various journals on line and in print. She is delighted to be included in this important collection.

Jim Cohn (44, 47), one of the "heart son" poets of Allen Ginsberg, played a significant role in the American Sign Language poetry revolution of the 1980s and is curator of the virtual Museum of American Poetics (poetspath.com), which he founded in Colorado in 1998. He is currently completing work on a singular compilation of his best and most lasting poetry, *Treasures for Heaven*.

Deborah Coy (13) has published three books and has been published in several anthologies and online poetry publications. She was an editor for the anthology, *La Llorona*, published by Beatlick Press, which won the New Mexico/Arizona Book Awards for Anthology in 2013.

Susy Crandall (12) lives in Albuquerque, NM. She has had poems published in both editions of the *Fixed and Free Poetry Anthology, The Más Tequila Review, Adobe Walls*, and a small collection called Shadow *of the Snake*, as well as a local online venue called *Elbow Room Magazine*. She started writing to save her own life and writing continues to support that endeavor.

During the day, **Steven Deridder** (104) tutors reading and writing at Sylvan Learning Centers. At night, he is a poet with a passion for photography, currently on vacation from both to finish his first sci-fi novel. His work has most recently been published in *Enzigam, Pencil Marks, and Mo' Joe.*

Mary Dudley (52) received a master's degree in English from SUNY/Stony Brook before moving to Albuquerque, New Mexico, where she earned a Ph.D. in child development across cultures. She has worked with young children and their families for many years. Her poetry has appeared in numerous publications.

Jim Fish (102) spent his early years in Southwest Texas. In 1981, after five years at Rice University, five at Princeton University (where he received a Ph.D. in chemical engineering), one in Cuernavaca, Mexico, and three in California, Fish landed in Placitas. He is the winemaker at Anasazi Fields Winery, and frequent host of poetry readings there.

Michael C. Ford (98) has been publishing steadily, since 1970, and is credited with over 28 volumes of print documents, as well as approx. 60 spoken word tracks. His debut vinyl received a Grammy nomination in 1986 and his *Selected Poems* earned a Pulitzer nomination in 1998. Hen House Studios markets his CD project *Look Each Other in the Ears* [2014]. That document, in both vinyl and CD, features a stellar band of musicians, including surviving members of a 1960s theatre rock quartet most of you will remember as The Doors.

Caitlin Gildrien (92) is a writer, graphic designer, and farmer living at the feet of the Green Mountains of Vermont. You can find her at www.cattailcreative.com.

After more than 30 years as a writer, journalist and educator, **Vincent F. A. Golphin** (21) teaches and writes in Central Florida. His most recent book, *Grandma Found a Gecko*, an early reader, was published last year. In 2012, FootHills Publishing released *Ten Stories Down*, poems based on his experiences in Beijing, China. Earlier, FootHills published, *Like A Dry Land: A Soul's Journey through the Middle East,* inspired by a 2003 visit to Jordan.

Larry Goodell (60, 101): Poet of performance and page, raconteur of earth's debacle from human greed, satirist of government secrecy and local real estate development, pianist, song-writer, playwright, performance poetry organizer, native of Roswell (1935) and resident of Placitas since 1963, a life-long organic gardener and founder of duende press. See http://www.larrygoodell.com/ and http://www.granarybooks.com/collections/goodell/

Kenneth P. Gurney (99) lives in Albuquerque, NM, USA with his beloved Dianne. His latest collection of poems is *Stump Speech* (2015). He runs the poetry blog *Watermelon Isotope*. His personal website is at kpgurney.me.

Ceinwen E.C. Haydon (69): Ceinwen's stories have been published in *Fiction on the Web*, *Literally Stories*, *StepAway* and *Alliterati*. Her poems are published in *Poems to Survive in*, *Writers Against Prejudice*, and *I am not a Silent Poet*. She is studying for an MA in Creative Writing at Newcastle University, UK.

Jack Hirschman (73): His second *The Arcanes*, 900 pages (poems written and or rediscovered from 2006-2016), has just been published in the American language by Multimedia Edizioni of Salerno, Italy. It is available through aggiefalk@hotmail.com

Patrick Colm Hogan (38) is a professor in the Department of English at the University of Connecticut. He is the author of *The Death of the Goddess: A Poem in Twelve Cantos* (2Leaf Press, 2014), *The Culture of Conformism* (Duke UP, 2001), *Understanding Nationalism* (Ohio State UP, 2009), and other works.

Lalita Pandit Hogan (58) is Professor of English at the University of Wisconsin—La Crosse, and an Affiliate faculty of the Center for South Asia at the University of Wisconsin—Madison. Her book of poems, *A Country Without Borders: Poems and Stories of Kashmir*, is forthcoming with 2Leaf Press, and she has numerous academic publications on a variety of subjects.

Back in 2008, **Catherine Iselin** (20) started writing poetry in Pat Schneider's writing workshop (Amherst Writers & Artists). She has continued writing poems ever since.

The poetry of **Mary Strong Jackson** (4) has appeared in journals and anthologies in the Unites States and England. Her chapbooks include *The Never-Ending Poem, Witnesses, No Buried Dogs, Between Door and Frame,* and *Clippings. From Other Tongues* is forthcoming in 2017. Read more of her work on strongjacksonpoet.wordpress.com. Mary recently moved from the high desert of Santa Fe, New Mexico to the green expanses of watery Wisconsin.

Kitty Jospé (87) completed her MFA in poetry at Pacific University in 2009 and has published 4 books. Her poems appear in *Nimrod, Grasslimbs, Poetrybay, Centrifugal Eye, Vehicle* and multiple anthologies. For her, poetry is an effective art for channeling words to carry meanings that strike at the heart.

Kathamann (64) is a returned Peace Corps Volunteer/Afghanistan and a retired registered nurse. She has been active in the Santa Fe arts community for 30 years, exhibiting in juried, group and solo exhibits (kathamann.com). Her poems have been published in local and regional anthologies.

Alan Kaufman (94) Alan Kaufman's memoir *Jew Boy* will be reissued this fall from Cornell University Press. The editor of *The Outlaw Bible of American Poetry*, he will tour this summer with Liberty Circus to raise funds for refugees and immigrants. www.libertycircus.com

Mary Ellen Kelly (23) enjoys her retirement from community college teaching through writing, photographing, and volunteering. Writing poetry in November of this year to help raise funds for the Center for New Americans, the organization in her Massachusetts community that welcomes immigrants, gave her a way to shout out against post-election despair and to connect with the hope inherent in creative acts.

Michael Ketchek (22) lives in Rochester NY, likes baseball, dark beer and haiku. Also likes chocolate and brandy, especially when hiking in the woods.

Stephen Lackow (27) was born in East New York, Brooklyn and has published in *American Poetry Review* and a number of little magazines. He studied several years with John Ashbery at Brooklyn College, and was a roommate of David Wojnarowicz and Janine Pommy Vega in Brooklyn Heights.

Gayle Lauradunn (63) produced a debut poetry collection, *Reaching for Air*, that was named a Finalist for Best First Book of Poetry by the Texas Institute of Letters. She has a second poetry collection forthcoming from FootHills Publishing, and her pocket-size chapbook *Duncan Canal, Alaska* is forthcoming from Grandma Moses Press. Her life has been devoted to social justice activism. She still hopes it has not been in vain.

Ezra E. Lipschitz (50) was born in 1955, then mostly raised in Colma, California. He completed a degree in English at U. C. Davis, but doesn't recall getting his diploma. This is his first publication, included in his first book, *I Shouldn't Say* (Mezcalita Press, LLC., 2017).

Douglas Lipton (25) was born and educated in Glasgow. He has spent most of his working life in Dumfriesshire as an English Teacher, Special Educational Needs Teacher and FE college Educational Support Worker. He began writing poetry in his teens, and attended the famed Glasgow University Department of Extra Mural and Adult Education Creative Writing Class inaugurated by Philip Hobsbaum.

A Pushcart and Best of the Net nominee, **Bobbie Lee Lovell** (8) placed twice in the Wisconsin Fellowship of Poets' 2016 Triad Contest. She believes her two children — and all children — deserve leaders who yearn to build bridges, not walls. Learn more at bobbieleelovell.com.

Dennis Maloney (70) is a poet and translator. A number of volumes of his own poetry have been published, including *The Map Is Not the Territory: Poems & Translations* and *Just Enough*. His book *Listening to Tao Yuan Ming* was recently published by Glass Lyre Press. A bilingual German/English, *Empty Cup* will appear in Germany in 2017. His works of translation include *The Stones of Chile* by Pablo Neruda, and *Between the Floating Mist: Poems of Ryokan*. He is also editor/publisher of the widely respected White Pine Press in Buffalo, NY.

Djelloul Marbrook (7) is the author of five books of fiction and four of poetry. His first poetry book, *Far from Algiers*, won the 2007 Stan and Tom Wick Poetry Prize from Kent State University. His next book, *Riding Thermals to Winter Grounds*, will be published in late winter 2017 by Leaky Boot Press, UK.

Teresa Mei Chuc (3) is the author of two collections of poetry, *Red Thread* (Fithian Press) and *Keeper of the Winds* (FootHills Publishing). Her chapbook of poetry is *How One Loses Notes and Sounds* (Word Palace Press). She is editor of the poetry anthology, *Nuclear Impact: Broken Atoms in Our Hands*.

The poetry **of David Morse** (59) has appeared in *California Quarterly*, *Crab Creek Review*, *Friends Journal*, *The Kerf* (nominated for a Pushcart Prize), *Potomac Review*, *Tiger's Eye*, and elsewhere. He is the author of a novel, *The Iron Bridge* (Harcourt Brace), and essays that have appeared in *Esquire*, *Green Mountains Review*, *The Nation*, *The New York Times Magazine*, and elsewhere. he lives in rural Connecticut, is busy restoring an old house and writing poems, and remains an activist on behalf of human rights and the local watershed.

The poems of **Bill Nevins** (107) have appeared in many anthologies and magazines. He has read at venues like the Maple Leaf (New Orleans), Bowery Poetry Café (NYC), and Taos Poetry Circus (NM). A collection of poems, *Heartbreak Ridge*, was published in 2014 by Swimming with Elephants. He is featured in the 2007 documentary *Committing Poetry in Times of War*. He lives in Albuquerque.

Maril Nowak (9) lives in the middle of New York State, the middle of nowhere, trying to imagine the middle, left, and right of Somewhere Else who voted for The Bloviator. She takes great comfort in Mencken's words. Americans survived Warren Harding, the original bloviator; we will survive this one too.

Jules Nyquist (72) is the founder of Jules' Poetry Playhouse, LLC, a place for poetry and play in Albuquerque, NM where Jules teaches poetry classes and hosts visiting writers. She took her MFA in Writing and Literature from Bennington College, VT. Jules' poems have appeared in *5 AM, Salamander, Malpais Review, Adobe Walls, A View from the Loft, St. Paul Almanac, Gray Sparrow, House Organ, Duke City Fix, Café Review* and others. Her website is www.julesnyquist.com

Stuart A. Paterson (26) is an award-winning, widely published & anthologised Scottish poet living on the Galloway coast. His latest publication is *Aye* (Tapsalteerie Press 2016), his first Scots language collection. For nearly 30 years he's been actively supporting the campaign for Scottish independence. *Looking South*, poems about Galloway, will be published by Indigo Dreams in 2017, and a CD of readings & songs in Scots will soon be released by Scotsoun Recordings. https://en-gb.facebook.com/patersonpoetry/

Don Paul (110) is the author of more than 25 books and the leader or producer of 23 albums. Many are available through New Orleans' Louisiana Music Factory. His most recent musical collaborations are with the GALLOP Trio and the Rivers of Dreams band. His website is donpaulwearerev.com

Poems by **Terez Peipins** (48) have appeared in publications both in the United States and abroad including *Anak Sastra, Barcelona Ink, Barcelona Review, Buffalo News, Conte, Kentucky Review, Melusine, and Pedestal,* among many others. She is the author of three chapbooks of poetry. Her novel, *The Shadow of Silver* Birch is published by Black Rose Writing. She won the 2016 Natasha Trethewey Prize in poetry from the Atlanta Writers Club.

Michael Peters (77) is the author of *Vaast Bin* and other assorted language art works. As certain as he is uncertain of access to "the real," Peters frequently probes this periphery in a variety of old and new media, utilizing sound-imaging strategies as something like a poet, a visual poet, a fictioneer, an essayist, an ecologist, a musician, and a programmer.

Colleen Powderly (45) began writing poetry in 1997. Early poems reflected her childhood in the deep South and years spent in the Midwest. Those poems eventually formed the basis for her book, *Split*, published by FootHills Publishing in 2009. More recent work has focused on stories from the working class, particularly from women's lives.

Randy Prus (43, 66): American politics died with John Quincy Adams, the greatest and least productive president in our history, ushering in American nationalism and its empire. I write in its shadow.

Sylvia Ramos Cruz (67) is a mother, grandmother, surgeon, women's rights activist, gardener, world traveler, friend and lover. Her poems, eclectic in form and content, are inspired by works of art in all its forms, women's lives, and every-day injustices. She loves words and what they can do.

Margaret Randall (97): Her most recent book of poems is *She Becomes Time* (Wings Press, 2016). Duke University Press published her bilingual anthology of eight decades of Cuban poetry, *Only the Road / Solo el camino* in the same year, and they published her *Exporting Revolution: Cuba's Global Solidarity* in Spring 2017. A new collection of poems, *The Morning After: Poetry & Prose in a Post-Truth Era*, will soon be out from Wings Press.

John Roche (1, 49, 116) is the author of *On Conesus, Topicalities, Road Ghosts, and The Joe Poems: The Continuing Saga of Joe the Poet*, as well as the author of *Mo' Joe: The Anthology*. He believes we are going to need poetry to get through the next four years or forty years.

Michael Rothenberg (32) is the editor of BigBridge.org and co-founder of 100 Thousand Poets for Change. His most recent book of poems is *Drawing the Shade* (Dos Madres Press, 2016). *Wake Up and Dream* will be published in spring 2017 by MadHat Press. He currently lives in Tallahassee, Florida.

Rudy Rucker (80) is a mathematician, a beatnik, and the author of twenty-three novels and sixteen other books. He received Philip K. Dick awards for his cyberpunk novels *Software* and *Wetware*. Other standouts are the novels *Postsingular* and *Turing and Burroughs*, as well as his nonfiction books *Infinity and the Mind* and *The Fourth Dimension*.

Ed Sanders (113, 114) has recently completed a long Investigative Poem called *Broken Glory, The Final Years of Robert Kennedy*, illustrated by Rick Veitch. He lives in Woodstock with his wife, Miriam, a painter and essayist.

Gretchen Schulz (37) is an Activist Artist at Large.

Patricia Roth Schwartz (57) is a poet and writer from New York's Finger Lakes. Widely published in small press journals, she has seven books of poems, including *Charleston Girls, a Memoir in Poems of a West Virginia Childhood*, and *The Crows of Copper John, a History of Auburn Prison in Poems*. From 2001 to 2015, she facilitated an inmates' poetry workshop inside Auburn Correctional Facility, a men's maximum security prison.

Gino Sky (95) is the author of fifteen books stories, poetry & novels, including *Appaloosa Rising: The Legend of the Cowboy Buddha*. During the Sixties he co-edited the literary magazine *Wild Dog*, considered by the NY Public Library one of the "finest underground mimeo magazine from the 1950's & 60's." He currently lives in Salt Lake City where he continues to write, draw, and maintain a woodworking shop.
Cowboy Buddha Press: cowboybuddhahotel@gmail.com

Jared Smith (39): His 13th volume of poetry, *Shadows Within the Roaring Fork*, will be published in Oregon by Flow Stone Press this summer. He is Poetry Editor of *Turtle Island Quarterly* and he now resides in the foothills of The Rockies, right outside Boulder, Colorado. His website, with more information, is www.jaredsmith.info

Jack Bradigan Spula (53) is a retired but not retiring pianist, poet and social activist in his home bioregion of the Eastern Great Lakes. He's working on the ground against Trumpism in Rochester, NY, and beyond.

Eugene Stelzig (34) is Distinguished Teaching Professor of English Emeritus at SUNY Geneseo. His poetry has appeared during the past six decades in a variety of little and literary magazines. He has also published two collections: *Fool's Gold: Selected Poems of a Decade* (FootHills, 2008), and *Assorted Selfscriptings 1964-1985* (Milne Library, SUNY Geneseo, 2015).

Eleanor Grogg Stewart (24) was a classical actress with an MA in theater. When she came to NM in 1970, her trickle of poems became a flood, and she published some of them in *Falling into Enchantment* in 2014. She taught English comp at UNM and also published a book, *Not Only a Refugee*, about teaching English at a Vietnamese refugee camp in the Philippines. She is currently working on a book of poems called *She Tells Us Stories*.

George Wallace (5, 6) is writer in residence at the Walt Whitman Birthplace, first poet laureate of Suffolk County LI, NY and author of 30 chapbooks of poetry, including *A Simple Blues with A Few Intangibles* (Foothills Publishing 2016).

Denise Weaver Ross is an artist, poet and graphic designer who lives and works in Albuquerque, New Mexico. Her images are richly layered with cultural, political, and historical references. Denise graduated from UMass–Amherst with a Master of Fine Arts degree, regularly exhibits in the Southwest, and contributes her design abilities to local writers, artists and galleries. Her art and poetry can also be found in many in local and international magazines and anthologies.

A former shop steward, and tool grinder, **Joe Weil** (65, 112) currently lives in Binghamton, NY and teaches at Binghamton University. His latest book is *A Night in Duluth*, published by New York Quarterly books in 2016.

Fred Whitehead (46, 109) is co-editor of an anthology, *Freethought on the American Frontier* (Prometheus, 1992), and editions of the poetry of Don Gordon and Vincent Ferrini from the University of Illinois Press. He lives in Kansas City, Kansas.

Scott Wiggerman (36) is the author of three books, *Presence, Leaf and Beak: Sonnets*, and *Vegetables and Other Relationships*; and editor of *Wingbeats: Exercises & Practice in Poetry, Lifting the Sky: Southwestern Haiku & Haiga*, and *Bearing the Mask*. Recent poems have appeared in *A Quiet Courage, Naugatuck River Review, Red Earth Review, bosque, shuf,* and *Yellow Chair Review*. He is an editor for Dos Gatos Press of Albuquerque, NM.

Holly Wilson (62) lives in Albuquerque, New Mexico, where she has been active in the poetry community for many years. She is one of the members of the Beatlick Sisters, a multimedia performance poetry duo. Politics is one of her favorite topics to talk and write about.

A. D. Winans (96) is an award-winning native San Francisco poet and writer. He is the author of over sixty books of poetry and prose. He edited and published Second Coming Press for 17 years. In 2006 he won a PEN Josephine Miles Award for excellence in literature. In 2009 PEN Oakland presented him with a Lifetime Achievement Award. In 2015 he was a recipient of a Kathy Acker Award in poetry and publishing.

Michael Young (iv) is a noted artist who grew up in Kansas, studied in NYC at the Art Students' League, the Salmagundi Club, and with anatomist Bill Weltman. He now lives in Kansas City, painting in a style he calls "Prismatism." His works have been exhibited throughout the nation.

Neil Young (108) hails from Belfast and now lives in north-east Scotland, where he is co-founder of *The Poets' Republic* magazine. His first collection, *Lagan Voices,* was published in 2011 (Scryfa), followed by *The Parting Glass - Fourteen Sonnets* (Tapsalteerie) in 2016. A new slim volume, *Jimmy Cagney's Long-Lost Kid Half-Brother*, will be published in May 2017 (Black Light Engine Room).

BEATLICK PRESS

Writers with Something to Say
Beatlick Press was established in 2011 to honor the memory of Beatlick Joe Speer of Albuquerque, NM and to continue his artistic mission to publish deserving writers.

Pamela Adams Hirst, publisher
Beatlick Press
Albuquerque, NM
http://beatlick.com/

&

JULES POETRY PLAYHOUSE PUBLICATIONS

Jules Nyquist is the founder and operator of Jules' Poetry Playhouse, LLC in Albuquerque, NM, a place for poetry and play
http://www.julesnyquist.com